TRADE AMONGST GROWING ECONOMIES

TRADE AMONGST GROWING ECONOMIES

IAN STEEDMAN

Professor of Economics
University of Manchester

CAMBRIDGE UNIVERSITY PRESS
CAMBRIDGE
LONDON · NEW YORK · MELBOURNE

Published by the Syndics of the Cambridge University Press
The Pitt Building, Trumpington Street, Cambridge CB2 1RP
Bentley House, 200 Euston Road, London NW1 2DB
32 East 57th Street, New York, NY 10022, USA
296 Beaconsfield Parade, Middle Park, Melbourne 3206, Australia

First published 1979

Printed in Great Britain by
Redwood Burn Ltd, Trowbridge and Esher

Library of Congress Cataloguing in Publication Data
Steedman, Ian.
Trade amongst growing economies.
Includes index.
1. Commercial policy. 2. Commodity control.
I. Title. II. Series.
HF1401.S7   382'3   78-73818
ISBN 0 521 22671 6

TO MY PARENTS

PREFACE

Developments both within orthodox trade theory and outside it have suggested for some time that attempts should be made to build a rather different theory of international trade, a theory in which produced means of production, profits and accumulation feature prominently. The following essay is intended to contribute to the process of constructing such a theory of trade. The analysis which it presents is, for the most part, based on an extremely simple model of international trade, in order that the main thrust of the argument should stand out clearly; it need hardly be said, therefore, that certain important aspects of trade are not dealt with. At the same time, the reader is urged not to judge the analysis merely on the grounds of its simplicity, for some elements of that simplicity can readily be dispensed with—whilst others, of course, cannot. (Chapters 2 and 10 are particularly germane to the separation of the dispensable from the indispensable simplifications.) It may also be noted that the essential features of the theory of trade presented here do *not* include the particular 'closures of the system' used, these latter having been selected on grounds of expositional simplicity alone. It is hoped that the student will acquire from the following arguments not only a specific set of theoretical results — some the same as those of orthodox theory, some perhaps less familiar — but also a general approach to the analysis of trade, which can be adapted to specific problems and assumptions other than those considered below.

It was Jo Bradley, Gautam Mathur and Joan Robinson who, over the course of several years, gradually persuaded me to write this small book: if the labour of writing may sometimes have dimmed my appreciation of their persuasive powers, I gladly express my gratitude to them now. For their comments, criticisms and encouragement at various stages, I should like to thank C. J. Bliss, L. M. Briscoe, D. J. Coppock, C. L. Day, H. D. Evans, P. Garegnani and G. Mathur. I am especially indebted to M. C. Kemp, L. Mainwaring and, above all, J. S. Metcalfe, for their thorough reading of all the following chapters and even of several versions of them. I fear that none of the above-named can be held to share my responsibility for what follows.

I also wish to thank both Sheila Fenton and Miss Edith Gillett and her colleagues for their excellent typing of versions of this book.

August 1978   I.S.

CONTENTS

Preface   vii

1 THE OBJECT OF A THEORY OF TRADE   1
Trends in volume   1
Trends in commodity composition   2
Trends in regional composition   2
The Heckscher–Ohlin–Samuelson theory of trade   3
    The endowment of 'capital'   4
    Capital as value   4
    Growth   5
    Primary inputs and consumption   6
Conclusion   7

2 A FRAMEWORK OF ANALYSIS   8
Long-period equilibrium   8
Production   9
Technical progress   9
Comparative dynamics   10
Effective demand and employment   11
Technical conditions of production   12
Competition and mobility   13
The Classical tradition in trade theory   14
Primary inputs   14
Consumption   16
Conclusion   16
Appendix: Select Bibliography   17

3 THE CLOSED ECONOMY   19
Part I A very simple closed economy   19
    The technique of production   20
    Wages, profits and prices   20
    Consumption, growth and the allocation of labour   23
    Closing the system   25
Part II Some complications   26
    Fixed capital   27
    Alternative techniques of production   28
    Choice of technique and consumption output   31
    More than one consumption commodity   32
    The analysis of trade   34

4 THE PATTERN OF TRADE FOR A SMALL ECONOMY   35
The method of analysis   35

The competitive pressure to trade   36
The choice of specialisation   38
Further analysis of the choice of specialisation   39
The proximate determinants of specialisation   40
A modification to the above analysis   43
An alternative technique of analysis   45
Summary   48

5   THE GAIN FROM TRADE IN A SMALL ECONOMY   49
The consumption–growth frontier for an open economy   50
The consumption-optimal specialisation   52
The consumption optimality of trade   53
The gain from trade   54
Trade, consumption and growth with a given wage   56
Summary   58
A reader's guide   59

6   TARIFF POLICY IN A SMALL ECONOMY   60
Tariffs   61
Tariffs and the pattern of specialisation   65
Tariffs with a given wage rate   66
Tariffs and protection   67
A reminder   72
Tariffs and the gain from trade   73
Tariff revenue   74
Summary   75

7   NON-TARIFF POLICY IN A SMALL ECONOMY   77
Subsidies   78
An example   80
Taxes   82
    Taxes on production   82
    A consumption tax   84
    A tax on wages   85
    A tax on profits   86
Multiple exchange rates   87
Import quotas   90
Summary   92

8   SOME COMPLICATIONS   94
Choice of technique   94
    Different M_1 machines   94
    Different M_2 machines   97
Many commodities   98
Non-tradeable commodities   99
    M_2 non-tradeable   100
    M_1 non-tradeable   101
    C non-tradeable   103
    Trade in consumption commodities alone   105
Summary   108

9 A SIMPLE ANALYSIS OF INTERNATIONAL
  EQUILIBRIUM 109
  Equilibrium international prices 110
  Comparative advantage 111
  Two special cases 114
  Wages, profits and prices 116
    Given rates of profit 117
    The general case 118
  Equilibrium with given wage rates 119
    Some comparative dynamics 121
  Equilibrium with one growth rate, one wage rate given 122
  Equilibrium with given growth rates 123
  International allocation of labour 125
  Summary 128

10 INTERNATIONAL EQUILIBRIUM FURTHER
   CONSIDERED 130
   Consumption and growth 130
   The consumption-optimality of trade and the gain from trade 132
   Equilibrium with constant rates of unemployment 134
     The growth rate of the labour supply 135
     Equilibrium 136
     Comparison of international equilibrium with autarkic equilibria 138
   Tariffs and international equilibrium 139
     Further on trade policy 142
   Non-tradeable commodities 143
     M_2 non-tradeable 143
     M_1 non-tradeable 144
     C non-tradeable 145
   Many commodities, many countries, many techniques 146
     More machines 148
     Alternative processes of production 149
     Many consumption commodities 150
     Many countries 150
   Summary 152
   An invitation 153

   Subject index 155

1
THE OBJECT OF
A THEORY OF TRADE

A useful theory of international trade, while it can never capture all the myriad complexities of such trade, must necessarily focus on its major features. The principal trends in the volume and composition of world trade over recent decades are, fortunately, not difficult to discern, even though each single datum or series of data relating to trade is subject to significant error.

TRENDS IN VOLUME

It may be noted first that the volume of world trade has grown significantly faster than the volume of world output. Furthermore, with respect to both trade and output, manufactures have grown faster than primary products. A useful summary indication of these changes is provided by Table 1.1, which shows various volume indices for 1974, with 1960 = 100 in each case. As the authors properly point out, the table 'is intended to serve only as a broad indication of the overall changes in world production and trade'. While no great precision should be attributed to the index numbers presented, they are sufficiently different from one another to show clearly both the growing share of manufactures in trade and output and the growing share of international trade in all three types of production. (The table is taken from GATT, *International Trade*, 1975/76, p. 4; the quoted qualification appears on p. 188. Further bibliographical details of all

Table 1.1

	World exports	World commodity production	
Agricultural products	156	141	Agriculture
Minerals (including fuels and non-ferrous metals)	231	197	Mining
Manufactures	393	239	Manufacturing

works cited in either this chapter or the next will be found in the select bibliography at the end of chapter 2.)

TRENDS IN COMMODITY COMPOSITION

Not only has the share of manufactures in the volume of trade increased steadily but marked changes have occurred in the relative importance in trade of different types of manufactures. First, the importance of non-durable consumer goods, particularly clothing and textiles, has declined. Secondly, the proportion of manufactured exports accounted for by capital goods has increased dramatically; particularly fast growing in volume terms (though not always in value terms, due to their falling relative prices) have been exports of machinery, transport equipment and chemicals. Summarising the findings of his major study, *Industrial Growth and World Trade*, Maizels therefore concluded (p. 416) that 'there seems little doubt that in the final quarter of this century international trade in manufactures is likely to be largely, or even mainly, in the "development sector" of engineering and chemical products'.

TRENDS IN REGIONAL COMPOSITION

Since manufactures are now the dominant element in the exports of industrialised countries, it is to be expected that the growing role of manufactures in world trade has been associated with a corresponding growth in the importance of the industrialised countries. This is indeed the case. The share of total world exports accounted for by the non-industrialised countries, other than oil producers, has declined. At the same time, the share of the mutual trade of North America, Western Europe and Japan in the total value of world trade grew steadily, until in the early 1970s such 'intra-industrial' trade accounted for over 50 per cent of world trade in value terms. (International trade statistics generally aggregate the figures for the non-capitalist economies of Eastern Europe, China, etc., so that the industrialised and non-industrialised non-capitalist economies cannot be distinguished.) The large increases in the relative prices of oil and certain other primary products which then occurred caused a sharp reduction in this share in the *value* of trade but it would seem unlikely that the growth of the 'intra-industrial' share in the *volume* of world trade will be checked.

It is clear then, that a theory of capitalist trade should account for trade between growing economies, placing considerable emphasis on the role of manufactures and, in particular, the place of capital goods in trade and, of course, in production.

THE HECKSCHER–OHLIN–SAMUELSON THEORY OF TRADE

In recent decades the theory of international trade has been dominated by the (perhaps ill-named) Heckscher–Ohlin–Samuelson (HOS) theory. Yet this theory is not particularly well-suited to the analysis of trade in manufactured goods, including capital goods, amongst growing economies.

That the HOS theory is not entirely appropriate for the analysis of contemporary trade stands out most clearly when the theory is considered in its basic form, as set out, for example, in Samuelson's classic papers, of 1948 and 1949, on 'factor price equalisation'. (Other formulations will be considered below.) In this basic form of the HOS model, a country produces only two commodities, both consumption goods. No produced means of production (capital goods) are used, production being carried out directly by unassisted homogeneous labour and homogeneous land, the fixed supplies of both land and labour being fully employed. By assumption, no capital goods are produced or traded. Furthermore, since the supply of land in a country cannot grow, sustained, full employment, steady growth of the world economy is not possible, with constant relative prices, unless technical progress should happen, quite providentially, to 'save land' at a rate equal to the growth rate of the effective labour force. (While to allow for changing relative prices would introduce difficult questions concerning expectations.)

Unlike the barrier to sustained growth, the absence of produced means of production can, in one sense, be readily corrected within the analysis. As was shown by Samuelson (1953–54), for example, their introduction leaves the HOS analysis essentially unaltered, *provided that* the capitalists who organise and control the productive activities, into which the produced means of production enter as inputs, obtain no profit on the value of those produced inputs. Yet the proviso is essential and some of the fundamental theorems of HOS theory cease to hold once the existence of positive profits is admitted; see, for example, Metcalfe and Steedman (1977). Since we are concerned to analyse a world in which positive profits are obtained on the value of capital goods, it is the qualification, rather than the statement qualified, that is important.

The endowment of 'capital'

While the more careful presentations of HOS theory, such as those of Samuelson cited above, assume a country to be endowed with given quantities of labour and land, other (perhaps more frequent) formulations take the given endowments of a country to consist of labour and 'capital'. This endowment of 'capital' merits further scrutiny, since it plays a crucial role both in the basic HOS theorem on the pattern of trade between two countries and in determining whether both countries can be incompletely specialised in the trade equilibrium and thus whether the 'factor-price equalisation' theorem holds.

The traditional concept of 'capital', as opposed to land and labour, is that it consists of, or at the very least is embodied in, *produced* means of production. The 'capital' endowment found in many HOS analyses, however, is simply given in quantity, even in long-run equilibrium: it is an apparently homogeneous, malleable productive input: and often it does not consist of produced means of production, for the only productive sectors are frequently consumer goods sectors (see, e.g., Jones (1956–57), Lancaster (1957)).

One way to interpret this 'capital' endowment is obviously to say outright that it is not the traditional factor 'capital' at all but is simply the traditional factor, 'land', masquerading under another name. On this reading, one should simply strike out the term 'capital' whenever it occurs and replace it by 'land'; one would then be left with an analysis which clearly failed to deal with the crucial role of produced means of production.

Capital as value

There is, however, an alternative possible interpretation of the 'capital' endowment, namely as a given sum of *value*; the assumption is then that whatever concrete, physical form may be taken by the capital goods within an economy, their total value, in some standard, must be equal to the exogenously given 'capital endowment'. Such an interpretation clearly fits in well with the long-run equilibrium nature of all basic trade theory since, by the meaning of the term, such an equilibrium is one in which it is determined endogenously which specific capital goods exist.

It cannot be taken for granted, however, that the properties of the HOS analysis with a given endowment of capital value are precisely analogous to the properties of the basic version with a given endowment of homogeneous land. This for the simple reason that a 'capital value' cannot be defined other than in terms of relative prices, which are to be determined *within* the analysis. It is thus less than transparent what is to be meant by saying that a country has a given endowment of capital value: in what units is this endowment measured? how does it come to be *given* in terms of, say, rice but *not given* in terms of, say, sunflower oil (for the relative prices of rice and sunflower oil are to be determined within the analysis)? Even were these puzzles resolved, the question would remain whether, by analogy with the properties of the land-based analysis, the capital–labour intensity of production in each sector is inversely related to the rate of profit and whether the price of a more capital-intensive commodity always rises relative to that of a less capital-intensive commodity when the rate of profit increases. The question is critical, for the monotonic relations at issue together constitute the very heart of HOS theory.

Now it has been demonstrated conclusively, by many different authors, that the capital–labour ratio in any sector need not be inversely related to the rate of profit (see Garegnani (1970) and Pasinetti (1977) for useful presentations of this point). Nor need the relative price of the more capital-intensive of two commodities rise as the rate of profit increases. Thus the two central properties of the land-based HOS analysis cannot be transferred by analogy to the version based on an endowment of capital value. As is to be expected, then, some of the principal standard conclusions of the HOS analysis are actually invalid, when applied to the capital value endowment case; see Metcalfe and Steedman (1973).

Thus it may reasonably be said that HOS theory fails to deal with the role of produced means of production (whether circulating or fixed capital goods), despite their evident and increasing importance: see Bhagwati (1964).

Growth

It is, consequently, not surprising, given the links between capital, profits and growth, that that theory has had relatively little to say about the persistent growth of output and trade: the majority of HOS analyses of 'growth' have been concerned with comparative statics results relating to the effects of a once-for-all increase in some exogenously given factor, e.g. labour supply. More recently, of course, a treatment of endogenous growth and trade has been developed within the HOS framework but it is not entirely satisfactory, for much of this literature is concerned with the transition to long-run equilibrium, starting from an arbitrary 'capital–labour' ratio, in models assuming a single capital good which can be combined with labour according to a neo-classical production function. (See the select bibliography for references.) It has yet to be shown that such analyses give real insight into the long-run equilibrium properties of the multi-capital-good models which must be developed to deal with real-world problems.

Primary inputs and consumption

Whilst the HOS analysis is less than fully satisfactory in its treatment of capital and of accumulation, it does—at least in its basic (land endowment) form—focus attention on the roles of primary, non-produced inputs and of consumer behaviour in the determination of international trade. Since neither primary input endowments nor consumption behaviour will feature at all prominently in the analysis presented below, it might be thought that the latter analysis and the HOS analysis are thus neatly complementary, each emphasising what the other leaves undiscussed.

Yet while the basic HOS theory certainly emphasises the role of relative endowments of land and labour, it does not provide an adequate account of the influence of natural resources on patterns of output and trade. The basic assumption is that both land and labour are homogeneous, both within each country and as between countries. The assumption that there are only two kinds of primary input can, of course, be relaxed but only at the cost of losing the real force of the basic concepts of *relative* endowments and *relative* factor intensities. More importantly, the assumption that primary inputs are qualitatively homogeneous as between countries precisely rules out serious consideration of the real influence of natural resources on trade flows. It must also be remembered that the root idea of the basic HOS theory, that the rent–wage ratio is, *ceteris paribus*, inversely related to the land–labour ratio, is invalid as soon as there is a positive rate of profit on the value of produced means of production; see Metcalfe and Steedman (1972). Thus, appearances notwithstanding, HOS theory does not provide a satisfactory analysis of natural resources and their effects on trade.

Again, although the HOS theory might appear to say much about the influence of consumption on production and trade, that appearance is perhaps deceptive. It is assumed, first, that all consumers in the world have identical preferences. It is then assumed, *in addition*, either that the common preference curves are homothetic or that, within each country, the structure of ownership of primary inputs is such that personal income shares are independent of relative primary input prices. It is well-established, within the HOS literature itself, that, unless these assumptions are made, HOS theory can say little about the pattern of production and trade. Few writers, therefore, would seriously maintain that that theory provides genuine knowledge about the influence of consumption behaviour on trade.

Thus while it is a merit of analyses within the HOS tradition that they oblige the reader to consider the question of how primary input endowments and consumption behaviour influence trade, it cannot be said that such analyses provide the corresponding answers.

CONCLUSION

It may be concluded that the HOS theory does not provide a firm foundation for the analysis of contemporary international trade. Authors working within the HOS tradition have themselves made very clear the difficulties which arise from unequal numbers of commodities and primary inputs, from 'factor intensity reversals', from increasing returns to scale, from non-identical preference patterns, and so on. When account is also taken of the need to give produced means of production, profits and growth a prominent role in the theory of trade, it would appear that an alternative framework for that theory should be sought.

2
A FRAMEWORK OF ANALYSIS

Before our detailed analysis is commenced in chapter 3, it will be well to set out here the general background assumptions and the analytical procedures which will inform the ensuing work. The reality of contemporary trade amongst growing economies is, it need hardly be said, highly complex and the reader will not expect that all its aspects will be captured by the theory presented below. Our analysis is based on the selection of simplifying assumptions which are judged to capture some of the strategic determinants of the object of investigation. No theory can do more. The analysis developed in this work does indeed focus attention on certain important relationships and determinations bearing upon central aspects of contemporary international trade; it is no less true that some important facets of such trade are not dealt with. The purpose of the present chapter is to set before the reader a clear statement of some of the major features, both positive and negative, of the work which follows. It is no part of the proper exposition of a theory to stress its strengths and to remain silent on its lacunae; both should be displayed, in order that the reader may form a reasoned assessment, acknowledging such insights as the theory may provide whilst recognising that they necessarily constitute less than the whole truth.

LONG-PERIOD EQUILIBRIUM

The simplest and most powerful tool for the analysis of the properties of an economy in which produced means of production are used is the method of long-period equilibrium. By definition, a long-period equilibrium displays the methods of production, the inputs, the outputs and the prices consistent with the existence of a uniform rate of profit. Since all inputs are variable in the long period, the quantities of all inputs, including the quantities of the various capital goods, are *endogenously* determined in such an equilibrium.

While a long-period equilibrium is certainly an analytical device, rather than a description, it is not an arbitrary device. On the contrary, it reflects the real and strong forces at work in a competitive, capitalist economy, which constantly tend to produce a uniform rate of profit, as capitalists unceasingly re-allocate their money capital in search of the highest rate of return. The method of long-period equilibrium analysis will therefore be used throughout this work.

While the long-period equilibrium method may be used for the analysis of any economy, it has been seen in chapter 1 that the theorist of contemporary trade must be concerned with growing economies. The most general and powerful application of long-period analysis to a growing economy is undoubtedly that embodied in the von Neumann model (1945–46) of an economy which is always in long-period equilibrium, with all physical quantities of positively priced goods growing at a common, constant rate. Each of the trade models presented below may properly be considered a special case of the von Neumann model (though always, it may be said at once, a very simple case). It follows, of course, that those models share both the strengths and the limitations of the general von Neumann model, as will be seen below.

PRODUCTION

While the pattern of consumption does play a role within von-Neumann-like models, since the long-period equilibrium depends on the proportions in which workers consume the various commodities, it is certainly the case that the *emphasis* is on the role of production and of produced means of production, rather than on consumption and consumer goods. Such an emphasis is clearly desirable in an analysis of trade which is concerned with economies experiencing continuous growth in their production and use of produced means of production. It has the further advantage that to stress production rather than 'consumer preferences' is to focus attention on *objective*, observable determinants of economic structure and thus on determinants about which something definite may be said.

It may be noted that, while much of the analysis will be presented in terms of a system with just three produced commodities, it will be seen in chapters 8 and 10 that an arbitrarily large number can readily be allowed for.

TECHNICAL PROGRESS

Since technical progress is an obvious and important feature of modern economic growth, it might reasonably be expected to feature prominently in the following analysis. Unfortunately, only its complete absence from the analysis will be noticeable. We shall be concerned with models of steady growth and, as is well known, the only type of technical progress which is generally consistent with such growth is purely 'labour-augmenting' progress, which is equivalent in its economic effects to a steady rise in the 'effective labour' done per worker-hour. It would be easy to allow for such technical progress, at many points in this work, but the restricted nature of the generalisation thus obtained would not appear to justify its explicit consideration. It will suffice to remark here that labour-augmenting (or Harrod-neutral) technical progress can be allowed for whenever an economy is undergoing steady growth with a given rate of profit. The corresponding constant real wage rate is then to be interpreted as an 'efficiency-wage', i.e. as a real wage in the ordinary sense which is growing at the rate of technical progress. In such a situation, the volume of employment will, of course, be growing less fast than output. Thus if trading economies, whose outputs grow at a common, constant rate, have different rates of Harrod-neutral technical progress, then the volume of employment will grow at a different rate in each country.

Since innovation is constantly changing both the available methods of production and the set of commodities produced, it has to be recognised that the failure to analyse technical progress constitutes a significant lacuna in this work.

COMPARATIVE DYNAMICS

As was stated above, albeit implicitly, the only growth paths considered will be steady growth paths, in which all positively priced physical quantities (employment, produced inputs, outputs) grow at a constant, common rate of growth, so that all proportions between physical quantities are constant over time. Such growth paths have been described, by Champernowne (1945–46), as paths of 'quasi-stationary' growth, for, while they capture the element of 'overall expansion' apparent in real world growth, they manifestly fail to describe the ever changing composition of inputs and outputs. Since it has been seen, in chapter 1, that world production and trade are not merely expanding but are changing in their commodity composition, steady growth analysis may seem inadequate for the study of contemporary trade. It is. Unfortunately, however, there is as yet no generally accepted method of analysing more complex growth paths, even in the context of closed-economy theory. We shall therefore use steady growth analysis, recognising its limited descriptive capacity and accepting it as an analytical device which may eventually be improved upon. (It may be noted that the assumption of steady growth at a positive rate is less restrictive than the assumption of steady growth at a zero rate, which is the assumption employed in much, though not all, HOS theory.)

An important aspect of the restriction to the analysis of steady growth paths is that one cannot trace out the *process* of adjustment to a change in any exogenous variable. One can only *compare* the steady growth path implied by the initial values of the exogenous variables with the steady growth path implied by the final values of those variables. This method of *comparative dynamics* will be used throughout. (It will be asked, for example, how the level of consumption per worker differs as between a trading and an autarkic economy with the same growth rate and identical available methods of production.) Thus processes of transition from one steady growth path to another will not be discussed: it may be noted, in particular, that the states of autarky and free trade (or restricted trade) will only ever be compared and no attempt will be made to analyse the process of adjustment from one such state to another. (To analyse such adjustment processes under the simplifying assumption that all heterogeneous capital goods, including used machines, can be costlessly transformed one into another, whether by production or by exchange on the world market, would be futile, since the limited possibility of such transformations is *central* to the problems of transition.)

EFFECTIVE DEMAND AND EMPLOYMENT

It is in the nature of steady growth analysis that no explanation is given of the absolute magnitude, at any given time, of outputs, inputs and employment levels. Such analysis explains only the relative sizes of such quantities—including, in the trade context, the *relative* sizes of the trading countries—and, if it is determined endogenously, the common rate of growth.

Effective demand considerations are, of course, taken account of, in that, by definition, along a steady growth path the relation 'intended net saving = actual net saving = actual net investment' is always satisfied (the government's budget and the external current account both being balanced). By the same token, however, 'effective demand considerations' relating to cyclical phenomena are not taken into account. Important as they are, the relations between fluctuations in international trade and 'domestic' employment cannot be analysed within the framework adopted throughout this work.

The preceding remarks must not be taken to mean that full employment of labour will always be assumed; it will not. Rather, full employment steady growth will be regarded as a very special case and, unless a full employment assumption is expressly stated, steady growth should be taken to mean 'steady growth in the presence of unemployed labour'.

It will *not* be assumed that the real wage rate must be zero when some labour is unemployed: the application to labour of the 'neo-classical rule of free goods' would involve a flight from reality too startling for even the steady growth theorist!

The various aspects of method mentioned so far bear no intrinsic relation to the international trade context of the present work; attention may now be turned to issues which do bear such a relation.

TECHNICAL CONDITIONS OF PRODUCTION

The assumption that technical conditions of production are identical as between trading economies can serve as a useful, expository device to bring out the effects on trade of influences other than technical conditions. Yet to make that identity a fundamental postulate of trade theory, as is done in HOS theory, is to refuse to discuss a major determinant of trade patterns.

It is trivial that the presumed spatial uniformity of the laws of nature does not entail the uniformity of the technical relations of production as between countries, where these relations encompass only selected, economically relevant and clearly specifiable inputs and outputs. All other relevant factors have to be treated as 'background' factors, whose influence is manifested precisely by the inter-country variation of technical conditions of production. Thus (often relevant) natural conditions, such as average annual temperature and humidity, differ between countries. No less important are many social differences. The technical knowledge actually available to those involved in production differs widely from country to country, as does scientific and technical experience. The levels and forms of labour skills and the forms of labour discipline at the point of production vary too, as do normal practices concerning shift working, etc.

Thus it will generally be assumed below that the prevailing, naturally and socially determined, technical conditions of production are not uniform as between countries.

COMPETITION AND MOBILITY

It will be assumed throughout that, *within* each country, labour and money capital are fully mobile between industries and that a uniform wage rate and a uniform rate of profit are thereby maintained. On the other hand, both labour and money capital will be assumed to be completely immobile as *between* countries, so that real wage rates and rates of profit can differ from one country to another. (Since technical conditions of production will not be assumed to be the same in all countries, the international mobility of commodities will not be found to imply international equality of either real wage rates or rates of profit.) It follows that 'labour' need not be homogeneous as between countries.

It will be clear that neither the assumption of 'internal' mobility nor that of 'external' immobility is to be regarded as a fully adequate reflection of real conditions; profit rate differentials do exist within countries, while very large flows of money capital take place between countries. A stable *structure* of relative rates of profit within any given country could, with only trivial effects, be incorporated within the following analysis but a proper treatment of international differences in profit rates could not be separated from that of international investment and it must be recognised that a full analysis of international capital and interest movements, and of their inter-relationships with trade flows, would be far more complex than the analysis presented below. The double assumption of internal mobility and international immobility, which is frequently made by trade theorists, will therefore be adopted as the best manageable simplification available.

It will be clear that the international immobility of money capital is perfectly consistent with the international mobility of capital goods. Indeed capital goods, like any other commodity, will be assumed to be traded on unified, competitive world markets. This is again an over-simplification, it need hardly be said, yet it is a reasonable first approximation, for it would be easy to exaggerate the importance of monopoly elements and of 'transfer pricing' on world markets. (It might even be argued that world markets are more competitive now than they have ever been.)

Since all external transactions other than trade will be ignored, as stated above, it must be assumed, in a steady growth analysis, that each country's trade is always balanced.

THE CLASSICAL TRADITION IN TRADE THEORY

The assumptions stated above concerning inter-country differences in technical conditions and the 'domestic' mobility of labour and money capital combined with their 'external' immobility will no doubt remind the reader of 'On Foreign Trade', the seventh chapter of Ricardo's *Principles of Political Economy and Taxation*. The analysis presented in this work does, indeed, have closer connections with what might be called the Classical tradition in trade theory—exemplified in such works as Ricardo (1951), Taussig (1927), Graham (1923), (1932), (1948), McKenzie (1953–54), (1954), (1955–56), Jones (1961)—than with the Neo-classical, or HOS, tradition. (It bears little relation, however, to what is commonly, if unfortunately, called 'Ricardian' trade theory in the textbooks, for that theory generally ignores the role of produced means of production, proceeds as if the rate of profit were zero, ignores the choice between alternative techniques of production and says nothing concerning growth.) It is therefore appropriate to consider the treatment of primary inputs and of consumption adopted below, since it is generally recognised that the Classical tradition does not stress the analysis of these issues. (As was noted in chapter 1, the HOS tradition does focus attention on such questions, albeit without providing the corresponding answers.)

PRIMARY INPUTS

The models of trade considered below involve, for a given country, only one primary input—homogeneous labour. Yet it is clear that no amount of emphasis on the importance of produced means of production can alter the facts that labour is not homogeneous, that land (in its traditional, broad sense) is not homogeneous and that land–labour endowments, broadly conceived, do influence patterns of production and trade. The fact that primary inputs are here collapsed to homogeneous labour thus requires discussion.

There would be little difficulty in allowing for the existence of different kinds of labour, provided only that the steady growth rate of output did not exceed the smallest of the various labour force growth rates. With a given wage rate for each type of labour, the single input and wage rate considered below would merely have to be replaced by a number of labour inputs and their respective wage rates. Indeed, in the case in which commodities enter all wage bundles in the same proportions and in which relative wage levels for different types of labour are given, no modification at all would be necessary: the analysis given below need only be re-interpreted, the single wage rate being taken as an index of the level of each wage rate and the labour input to a production process being an appropriately weighted sum of the various specific labour inputs. Thus the following analysis could, in effect, be taken to refer to any number of different types of labour, subject to the fairly strong assumption of exogenously given relative wage rates.

Turning now to natural resources, we may note that there is some force in the argument (see Caves and Jones (1973), p. 1) that the role of natural resources will often be so transparent that no theory is required to aid one's understanding of it. Thus it is trivially true that if a nation's territory includes no tin deposits then tin ore will not be exported from that country. Yet such obvious truths, while not to be ignored, do not take one far: e.g., if a nation's territory does include tin deposits then those deposits may or may not be worked, if they are worked the ore may be exported or processed domestically, and so on. Thus even if it be true that the effects on trade of natural resources are sometimes obvious and even though the importance in world trade of (non-oil) natural resource based exports is declining, it remains the case that the role of natural resources must be examined.

The existence both of land in the narrow sense (the area of soil with its 'original and indestructible powers') and of exhaustible resources (such as minerals and fossil fuels) clearly rules out the possibility of *perpetual* steady growth at a positive rate, at least in the absence of appropriate technical progress. Yet it is compatible with such growth as long as no land of any given quality is fully used and as long as the (eventually) exhaustible resources can be extracted at constant costs. It will be assumed throughout that these conditions do indeed hold good in each country, all rents being zero. Natural resource endowments, which are assumed to differ between countries both in relative quantity and in quality, will nevertheless play a role in the analysis since, as has been stated above, they help to determine the different technical conditions of production in the various countries.

CONSUMPTION

As has been stated above, the role of production, rather than that of consumption, will be emphasised throughout this work. Thus it will often, although not always, be assumed that there is only one kind of consumption commodity. When many kinds are allowed for, they will generally be assumed to enter consumption in fixed proportions, so that it is as if there were a single consumption commodity. This apparently cavalier treatment of consumption may be justified first on the procedural ground that one may reasonably treat in the simplest way an issue which is not the major focus of attention. More significantly, since it might be objected that consumption behaviour ought to be a dominant concern in trade theory, it may be justified on the ground that there is little that can usefully be said about the determinants of consumption at a given level of *per capita* income. Consumer 'preferences' are intangible and may be employed as a *deus ex machina* to explain anything—and thus nothing. Again, little can be said concerning the effects of differences in relative prices on aggregate consumption patterns, since relative price differences are inextricably related to differences in income distribution. It is thus reasonable to treat the proportions in which consumption commodities are consumed as exogenously determined, admitting that one cannot explain them.

CONCLUSION

The reader will not mistake the theory of trade presented below for a fully adequate account of all important aspects of contemporary growth, production and trade. It may, nevertheless, provide a simple, coherent framework within which certain important facets of contemporary international trade can usefully be interpreted and understood and it is not unreasonable to hope that some, at least, of the limitations of that simple framework could be removed without destroying the essential thrust of the argument given below.

It will be found throughout that the principal proximate determinants of the international division of labour, of the pattern and magnitudes of trade flows and of international and domestic prices are the technical conditions of production in each country (as determined by the prevailing natural conditions and by the country's whole social and economic history), income distribution and the strength of the capitalists' urge to accumulate.

APPENDIX: SELECT BIBLIOGRAPHY

Of the various specialised branches of economic theory, international trade theory must have one of the most extensive literatures and the following bibliography does not provide even a representative selection of the works in that field. Rather, it contains only the full references to the works alluded to in this and the previous chapter, together with a number of other works having an immediate bearing on the type of theory presented in this book. (The reader requiring a lengthy bibliography on pure trade theory may be referred to the outstanding survey by Chipman, cited below.)

(a) Trends in world trade

GATT. *International Trade*, Geneva, annual.
A. Maizels. *Industrial Growth and World Trade*, Cambridge, 1971.
P. L. Yates. *Forty Years of Foreign Trade*, London, 1959.

(b) Basic trade theory

J. Bhagwati. 'The Pure Theory of International Trade: A Survey', *Economic Journal*, 1964.
J. Bhagwati (ed.). *Penguin Readings in International Trade*, Harmondsworth, 1969.
R. E. Caves. *Trade and Economic Structure*, Harvard, 1960.
R. E. Caves and R. W. Jones. *World Trade and Payments*, Boston, 1973.
J. S. Chipman. 'A Survey of the Theory of International Trade', *Econometrica*, 1965 and 1966.
R. W. Jones. 'Factor Proportions and the Heckscher–Ohlin Theorem', *Review of Economic Studies*, 1956–57.
M. C. Kemp. *The Pure Theory of International Trade and Investment*, New Jersey, 1969.
K. Lancaster. 'The Heckscher–Ohlin Trade Model: a Geometric Treatment', *Economica*, 1957.
P. A. Samuelson. 'International Trade and the Equalization of Factor Prices', *Economic Journal*, 1948.
'International Factor-price Equalization Once Again', *Economic Journal*, 1949.

(c) Growth within the HOS tradition

P. K. Bardhan. 'Equilibrium Growth in the International Economy', *Quarterly Journal of Economics*, 1965.
'On Factor Accumulation and the Pattern of International Specialisation', *Review of Economic Studies*, 1966.
K. Inada. 'International Trade, Capital Accumulation, and Factor Price Equalization', *Economic Record*, 1968.
H. G. Johnson. 'Trade and Growth: A Geometrical Exposition', *Journal of International Economics*, 1971. (See also, *ibid.*, 1972, for a correction.)
H. Oniki and H. Uzawa. 'Patterns of Trade and Investment in a Dynamic Model of International Trade', *Review of Economic Studies*, 1965.

(d) The Classical tradition

F. D. Graham. 'Some Aspects of Protection Further Considered', *Quarterly Journal of Economics*, 1923.
  'The Theory of International Values', *Quarterly Journal of Economics*, 1932.
  The Theory of International Values, Princeton, 1948.
R. W. Jones. 'Comparative Advantage and the Theory of Tariffs: A Multi-country, Multi-commodity Model', *Review of Economic Studies*, 1961.
L. W. McKenzie. 'Specialization and Efficiency in World Production', *Review of Economic Studies*, 1953–54.
  'On Equilibrium in Graham's Model of World Trade and Other Competitive Systems', *Econometrica*, 1954.
  'Specialization in Production and the Production Possibility Locus', *Review of Economic Studies*, 1955–56.
D. Ricardo. *On the Principles of Political Economy and Taxation*, Cambridge, 1951.
F. W. Taussig. *International Trade*, New York, 1927.

(e) Works bearing directly on the theory presented below

L. Mainwaring. 'A Neo-Ricardian Analysis of International Trade', *Kyklos*, 1974.
  'Relative Prices and "Factor Price" Equalisation in a Heterogeneous Capital Goods Model', *Australian Economic Papers*, 1976.
S. Parrinello. 'Introduzione ad una Teoria Neoricardiana del Commercio Internazionale', *Studi Economici*, 1970.
  'Distribuzione, Sviluppo e Commercio Internazionale', *Economia Internazionale*, 1973.
P. A. Samuelson. 'Trade Pattern Reversals in Time-phased Ricardian Systems and Intertemporal Efficiency', *Journal of International Economics*, 1975.
I. Steedman (ed.). *Fundamental Issues in Trade Theory*, London, 1979.
I. Steedman and J. S. Metcalfe. 'The Non-Substitution Theorem and International Trade Theory', *Australian Economic Papers*, 1973.
  '" On Foreign Trade" ', *Economia Internazionale*, 1973.

(f) Other works cited

D. G. Champernowne. 'A Note on J. von Neumann's Article on "A Model of Economic Equilibrium" ', *Review of Economic Studies*, 1945–46.
P. Garegnani. 'Heterogeneous Capital, the Production Function and the Theory of Distribution', *Review of Economic Studies*, 1970.
J. S. Metcalfe and I. Steedman. 'Reswitching and Primary Input Use', *Economic Journal*, 1972.
  'Heterogeneous Capital and the Heckscher–Ohlin–Samuelson Theory of Trade', in J. M. Parkin and A. R. Nobay (eds.), *Essays in Modern Economics*, London, 1973.
  'Reswitching, Primary Inputs and the Heckscher–Ohlin–Samuelson Theory of Trade', *Journal of International Economics*, 1977.
J. von Neumann. 'A Model of General Economic Equilibrium', *Review of Economic Studies*, 1945–46.
L. L. Pasinetti. *Lectures on the Theory of Production*, London and New York, 1977.
P. A. Samuelson. 'Prices of Factors and Goods in General Equilibrium', *Review of Economic Studies*, 1953–54.

3

THE CLOSED ECONOMY

While the principal purpose of this volume is, of course, to provide an analysis of open, trading economies, it will be helpful to follow the traditional and sensible practice of first analysing a closed economy in some detail. This procedure will enable the reader to grasp certain important economic relationships without, at first, having to allow for the complexities of international trade. Furthermore, the nature and significance of international trade may be more fully understood when the properties of an open, trading economy are compared with those of an otherwise similar closed, or autarkic, economy. Again following traditional practice, we shall first consider a particularly simple closed economy before turning attention to various complications. It will, of course, be understood that even once these complications have been introduced, the analysis will not be that of a fully 'realistic' model of the economy. The only claim to be made is that our analysis will focus attention, in a sharp and simple way, on *some* important features of real economies.

PART I A VERY SIMPLE CLOSED ECONOMY

Consider a closed, capitalist economy in which there are just two social classes, the capitalists, who perform no labour, and the workers, who own no property. There is no government. Only one consumption commodity is produced and there is only one available way of effecting that production. All productive processes exhibit constant returns to scale and there is no technical progress. Furthermore, all capital goods, i.e. all produced means of production, are fully used up in one annual cycle of production, so that there is no fixed capital. If these assumptions, like others to be made below, seem severe, it must be remembered that some of them, at least, will be relaxed later. (Thus the existence of many consumption commodities, of a choice of production methods and of durable capital goods will all be referred to below.)

The technique of production

Suppose there to be three produced commodities; the consumption commodity, C, the type of machine used in the production of C, machine M_1, and a second type of machine, M_2, which can be used to produce either machines of the first kind or further machines of the second kind. (The reader might like to think of C as corn, of M_1 as a tractor lasting one year, and of M_2 as a machine tool which lasts for one year.) Each production process requires as an input not only a machine of the appropriate type but also a quantity of the homogeneous labour, L, which is supplied by the workers. Table 3.1 shows the physical quantities of inputs to and outputs from each process, when it is operated by one unit of labour, for one year. It will be noted that one unit of labour always works with one machine and that, in particular, each machine of the second kind is operated by one unit of labour whether it is being used to make machines of the first type or machines of the second type.

Table 3.1

	Inputs			Outputs	
L	M_1	M_2	C	M_1	M_2
1	1	0	q	0	0
1	0	1	0	m_1	0
1	0	1	0	0	m_2

Wages, profits and prices

The relationships between the wage rate, the profit rate and relative prices will now be examined, under the assumption that, as a result of the inter-industry mobility of both labour and money capital, the wage rate and the profit rate are both uniform as between the different processes of production and that the profit rate obtained on each process is equal to that which was expected by the capitalists investing in it. Let the annual rate of profit be r; let the real wage rate, paid at the end of the year, be w and the price of machine M_i be p_i ($i = 1, 2$), where w, p_1 and p_2 are measured in terms of the consumption commodity. Then the following equilibrium relations must obtain:

$$w + p_1(1 + r) = q \qquad (1)$$

$$w + p_2(1 + r) = m_1 p_1 \tag{2}$$

$$w + p_2(1 + r) = m_2 p_2 \tag{3}$$

Equation (1), for example, states that the value of gross output, per unit of labour employed, in the consumption commodity process, q, *equals* the wage, w, *plus* the value of the machine used up, p_1, *plus* profit at the rate r on that machine value, rp_1. Equations (2) and (3) make analogous statements about the other two processes of production.

The three relations (1), (2) and (3) do not suffice to determine the four unknowns (w, r, p_1, p_2). The question how the system might be completed and the precise values of w, r, p_1 and p_2 thus be determined, will be considered below; here we shall simply examine how w, p_1 and p_2 vary as functions of the profit rate, r. In effect, then, r will be treated *as if* it were known and (1), (2) and (3) then used to determine w, p_1 and p_2. (It is not implied that r is actually 'given'; indeed, the analysis will subsequently be repeated treating w *as if* it were known.)

The wage–profit frontier. Consider first the relationship between the wage rate and the profit rate. On eliminating p_1 and p_2 from (1), (2) and (3), one finds that:

$$w = \left\{ \frac{m_1[m_2 - (1 + r)]q}{m_1 m_2 + (m_2 - m_1)(1 + r)} \right\} \tag{4}$$

This relationship, which, for given technical coefficients, shows the wage rate, w, as a function of the profit rate, r, will be referred to as the wage–profit frontier.

It is easy to show that the right-hand side of (4) always decreases when r increases, so that w and r are always inversely related; neither the wage rate nor the profit rate can increase except at the expense of the other. The wage–profit frontier is shown in Fig. 3.1, from which it will be seen

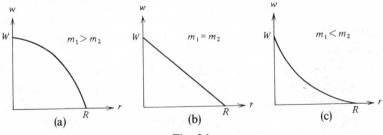

Fig. 3.1

that, while the frontier is always downward sloping, the curvature of the frontier depends on the relative magnitudes of m_1 and m_2.

When r is zero, the wage takes a maximum value, W, which can be found by setting $r = 0$ in (4). As r rises, w falls, until at the maximum possible profit rate, R, the wage is zero; it is clear from (4) that $(1 + R) = m_2$. It may be noted that, whereas the maximum wage depends on the technical coefficients of all three processes, the maximum profit rate depends only on the properties of the third process in Table 3.1 being, in fact, the rate at which machines of the second type can 'reproduce themselves', net of replacement.

It should be noted from (4) that when $r = -1, w = q$. This result is naturally of only formal significance, for capitalists will not invest if expecting a negative rate of return, but it will prove to be of use below.

Profits and prices.   It may now be considered how machine prices, p_1 and p_2, will depend on r. From (2) and (3) it follows immediately that:

$$m_1 p_1 = m_2 p_2$$

so that the ratio (p_1/p_2) is quite independent of r. The individual values of p_1 and p_2 do depend on r, however, according to the relations:

$$p_1 = \left[\frac{m_2 q}{m_1 m_2 + (m_2 - m_1)(1 + r)} \right] \tag{5}$$

$$p_2 = \left[\frac{m_1 q}{m_1 m_2 + (m_2 - m_1)(1 + r)} \right] \tag{6}$$

It will be seen from (5) and (6) that the way in which p_1 and p_2 vary as r varies is determined by the relative magnitudes of m_1 and m_2. If $m_1 = m_2 = m$, say, then

$$p_1 = p_2 = (q/m),$$

and machine prices are independent of r. On the other hand, if $m_1 > m_2$ then p_1 and p_2 both rise as r rises, while if $m_1 < m_2$ then p_1 and p_2 both fall as r rises.

(The result that p_1 and p_2 rise, remain constant or fall, as r rises, according as $m_1 \gtreqless m_2$, is intimately related to the earlier finding that the wage–profit frontier is bowed outwards, linear or bowed inwards according as $m_1 \gtreqless m_2$ (see Fig. 3.1). An investigation of that relationship would, however, serve no useful purpose here.)

Profits and prices with a given wage rate.   While w, p_1 and p_2 were shown above as functions of the profit rate, r, one could just as well derive r, p_1 and p_2 as functions of the wage rate, w, and indeed both approaches will prove of use below. The relations obtained are shown in (7), (8) and (9) and the reader may check that, *mutatis mutandis*, the discussion of the previous two sections can be repeated in terms of these relations.

$$(1 + r) = \left[\frac{m_1 m_2(q - w)}{m_1 q + (m_2 - m_1)w} \right] \tag{7}$$

$$p_1 = \left[\frac{m_1 q + (m_2 - m_1)w}{m_1 m_2} \right] \tag{8}$$

$$p_2 = \left[\frac{m_1 q + (m_2 - m_1)w}{m_2^2} \right] \tag{9}$$

Consumption, growth and the allocation of labour

The discussion so far has been concerned, almost exclusively, with relationships between wages, profits and prices. We now consider the relations that must hold between physical quantities, such as the allocation of labour to each production process and the level of the corresponding physical outputs. To do this it is very convenient to assume that the economy is undergoing steady growth, that is growth in which every physical input and output grows at the same, constant percentage rate per annum, so that all ratios between quantities remain constant. While convenient, this assumption is certainly not realistic; real world growth patterns are far more complex. Even for closed economies, however, the analysis of non-steady growth is not well developed, so that it would be quite out of place to attempt such an analysis in the present work. We shall therefore, albeit reluctantly, rest content with analysing international trade in the context of steady, or 'quasi-stationary', growth.

Consider then an economy growing at the steady percentage rate g; let L_c, L_1 and L_2 be the amounts of labour allocated to the C, M_1 and M_2 sectors, respectively and c, x_1 and x_2 be the outputs from those sectors, per unit of total employment in the economy. (With constant returns to scale and steady growth all *relative* quantities will be constant over time.)

Since outputs are defined relative to total employment, define

$$L_c + L_1 + L_2 = 1 \tag{10}$$

so that the Ls are, in effect, the *proportions* of total labour which are allocated to each sector. From Table 3.1 it may now be seen that the following relations must hold.

$$c = qL_c \tag{11}$$

$$x_1 = m_1 L_1 = (1+g)L_c \tag{12}$$

$$x_2 = m_2 L_2 = (1+g)(L_1 + L_2) \tag{13}$$

Equation (11) merely states that consumption is equal to the output of the consumption good sector. Equation (12) shows that output of the M_1 sector ($= x_1 = m_1 L_1$) must not only suffice to replace the L_c machines used up in the C sector but must also provide for the growth of the machines used in that sector. In the same way, (13) ensures that the output of the M_2 sector ($= x_2 = m_2 L_2$) can both replace and expand the supply of M_2 machines used in the M_1 and M_2 sectors.

The equations (10) to (13) do not suffice to determine all the variables but are adequate to determine each variable as a function of, say, g.

The allocation of labour.   It follows from equations (10), (12) and (13) that;

$$L_c = \left\{ \frac{m_1[m_2 - (1+g)]}{m_1 m_2 + (m_2 - m_1)(1+g)} \right\} \tag{14}$$

$$L_1 = \left\{ \frac{[m_2 - (1+g)](1+g)}{m_1 m_2 + (m_2 - m_1)(1+g)} \right\} \tag{15}$$

$$L_2 = \left\{ \frac{(1+g)^2}{m_1 m_2 + (m_2 - m_1)(1+g)} \right\} \tag{16}$$

Consider now how the proportional allocation of labour between the three industries varies, as g increases from zero to its maximum possible value of $(m_2 - 1)$. It follows from (14) and (16) that L_c falls monotonically to zero, while L_2 rises monotonically to unity. Thus the higher is the rate of growth, the smaller is the proportion of the labour force allocated to the production of the consumption commodity and the larger is the proportion allocated to producing the basic M_2 machine. As g rises, L_1 falls monotonically to zero if and only if $m_2 \geq m_1(m_2 - 1)^2$; otherwise, it rises at first and then falls to zero.

Since $x_i = m_i L_i (i = 1, 2)$, it will be clear that x_2 will be greater the higher is the rate of growth but x_1 may be greater or smaller with a higher growth rate.

The consumption–growth frontier. It follows from (11) and (14) that

$$c = \left\{ \frac{m_1[m_2 - (1+g)]q}{m_1m_2 + (m_2 - m_1)(1+g)} \right\} \tag{17}$$

This relation between consumption output per unit of employment, c, and the growth rate, g, will be referred to as the consumption–growth frontier. There is, fortunately, no need to analyse the properties of this relation, for if we compare it with the wage–profit frontier (4) it is apparent that the two frontiers are identical; (17) can be obtained from (4) by simply replacing w by c and r by g. Thus the previous demonstration that the frontier is downward sloping, with a curvature dependent on the relative sizes of m_1 and m_2, applies to the consumption–growth frontier as well. The reader may find it useful to re-read the relevant sections with this point in mind.

Closing the system

All that has been shown so far in this chapter is that the conditions of production determine certain *relations* between, on the one hand, wages, profits and prices and, on the other hand, physical outputs, growth and labour allocations. Nothing has been said about the determination of the particular values taken by any of the economic variables considered.

Savings behaviour. It will be assumed throughout this work that savings out of wages are zero, while capitalists wish to save a fraction $s(0 \leq s \leq 1)$ of their profits. In steady, equilibrium growth, net investment is equal not only to *ex post* net saving but also to *ex ante* net saving. Let the (positive) value of capital in any period be V. Then net investment equals gV, while *ex ante* net saving equals srV. Hence, in steady growth,

$$gV = srV$$

or
$$g = sr \tag{18}$$

Relation (18) does not yet close the system of relationships found above but it does at least provide a link between the wage–profit–price equations and the physical quantity equations.

A given wage rate. One way to close the system is to regard the wage in terms of the consumption commodity, w, as exogenously determined. The profit rate, r, is then determined, by (7), and hence the growth rate, g, is determined, by (18). Relative prices, labour allocations and physical outputs then follow from the appropriate equations above.

Taking the real wage rate as given—which may reasonably be labelled a 'classical' procedure, since it was adopted by Quesnay, Ricardo and Marx—does not involve assuming that it is given at a physiological 'subsistence' level, it should be noted. All that is involved is the assumption that the wage rate, however 'high' or 'low' it might be, is determined by forces which lie beyond the scope of the present analysis; though they may, of course, be amenable to analysis of another kind.

A given growth rate. An alternative closure of the system is provided by the assumption that the growth rate, g, is exogenously determined. The profit rate, r, is then determined, by (18), and hence the wage rate, w, is determined, by (4). Relative prices and the various physical quantities are then given by the appropriate relations above.

This assumption—which may be described as 'neo-Keynesian'—is usually related to the idea that the rate of growth is determined by the general level of dynamism and resourcefulness, or 'animal spirits', of the capitalists, these animal spirits themselves not being open to further economic analysis. (They may be open to further sociological and political analysis, however.)

It may be noted that while some writers would associate the 'classical' case of a given wage rate with the existence of unemployment and the 'neo-Keynesian' case of a given growth rate with the existence of full employment, no such rigid associations need be or will be made in this work.

While there are, of course, yet other ways of closing the system, it will be convenient here to confine attention to the two methods just stated, leaving to the reader the task of considering alternative closures of the system. It is important to note, however, that the general approach to the analysis of international trade which is presented in this work is independent of the adoption of any particular system closure. It follows that the reader's judgement of the acceptability of the general framework of analysis set out below is not to be based on an assessment of the particular system closures which are adopted for the purpose of expounding that framework.

PART II SOME COMPLICATIONS

The reader will not need to be reminded of the restrictive nature of the various assumptions made above; we now indicate how some of them, at least, may be relaxed, by considering the existence of fixed capital, alternative production methods and many consumption commodities. The 'consumption/growth' efficiency of the capitalist choice of technique will also be considered.

Fixed capital

It was assumed above that each type of machine was fully used up (or worn out) in one cycle of production, i.e. that there was no fixed capital. If we now make the 'opposite' extreme assumption, that no machine ever wears out, then we simply have to modify Table 3.1 to obtain Table 3.2; each machine appears both as an input to and an output from the production process. Note that Table 3.2 is exactly the same as Table 3.1 on the left-hand side and differs on the right-hand side only by the addition of one (M_1 or M_2) machine in each process.

Table 3.2

	Inputs			Outputs	
L	M_1	M_2	C	M_1	M_2
1	1	0	q	1	0
1	0	1	0	m_1	1
1	0	1	0	0	$m_2 + 1$

On writing down the wage, price, profit relations corresponding to (1), (2) and (3) above, one finds, after simplifying, that

$$w + p_1 r = q \tag{1'}$$

$$w + p_2 r = m_1 p_1 \tag{2'}$$

$$w + p_2 r = m_2 p_2 \tag{3'}$$

It will be seen that (1'), (2') and (3') differ from (1), (2) and (3) respectively only in that $(1 + r)$ has been replaced by r. It follows immediately that w, p_1 and p_2 may be found as functions of r simply by replacing $(1 + r)$ by r in (4), (5) and (6).

On the physical quantities side, equations (12) to (17) can be appropriately modified simply by replacing $(1 + g)$ by g.

More complex modifications would, of course, be required if one of the machines were assumed to wear out in one year, while the other were assumed to last for ever. Yet more complex is the proper analysis of systems in which machines wear out over several years, particularly if the efficiency of a machine depends on its age. In the interest of simplicity, therefore, attention will be confined below to the case of circulating capital but it should be borne in mind that, at the cost of greater complexity, the analysis could readily be adapted to deal with other cases.

Alternative techniques of production

It has been assumed so far that there is only one available technique for the (direct and indirect) production of the consumption commodity. It must now be shown how, if alternative techniques are available, the choice between them is made. It will suffice here to consider two types of alternative techniques; in the first case the two techniques differ only in using different machines for the production of the consumption commodity, while in the second case they differ only in having different 'M_2' machines. In each case our approach—which may readily be adapted to other cases—will be to find the wage—profit frontier for each technique and then to argue that that technique will be chosen which gives the higher profit (or wage) rate for the given wage (or profit) rate.

Techniques with different M_1 machines.   Suppose that in addition to the technique analysed above, call it T, defined by the parameters m_2, m_1 and q, there is an alternative technique, T', in which C is made by labour using an M_1' type machine, which is itself produced by the M_2 type machine. This technique will, of course, be defined by parameters m_2, m_1' and q'. The question now arises, which technique will be used, T or T'?

The analysis of this question is perhaps best shown by means of an example. Suppose that the production coefficients are:

$$\text{Technique } T \ : m_2 = 2, m_1 = 1, q = 7$$
$$\text{Technique } T' : m_2 = 2, m_1' = 2, q' = 4$$

On substituting the appropriate values into (4), one finds that the wage $w(w')$ for technique $T(T')$ is given by

$$w = \left[\frac{7(1-r)}{3+r} \right], w' = 2(1-r)$$

The two wage–profit frontiers are shown in Fig. 3.2. They intersect at $(w = w' = 1, r = 50\%)$ and at $(w = w' = 0, r = 100\%)$; that T and T' have

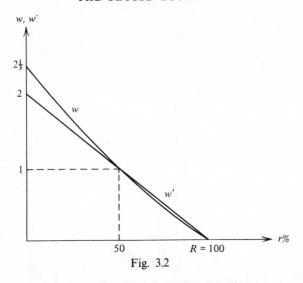

Fig. 3.2

the same maximum rate of profit ($R = 100\%$) follows from their having the same M_2 machine. Suppose that the real wage in terms of C is given exogenously. Then in a competitive economy capitalists will choose technique T if the wage exceeds unity, for at such a wage rate T gives the higher profit rate; at wage rates less than unity, however, they will choose technique T', for the same reason. On the other hand, if the growth rate, g, is given exogenously, so that r is determined through (18), then for profit rates of less than 50% technique T will be chosen, while for profit rates greater than 50% technique T' will be used.

The above example suffices to show that the wage–profit frontiers for two techniques, which differ only with respect to the type of machine used in producing C, can intersect at positive (r, w) so that the technique used depends on the level of the given wage rate or growth (and hence profit) rate. It is not implied that two such frontiers must necessarily intersect for positive (r, w); if one frontier dominates the other, then the same technique will be used whatever is the distribution of income.

It will be clear that the method of analysis is not restricted to the case of only two alternative techniques.

Techniques with different M_2 machines. Suppose now that, in addition to technique T defined by the parameters (m_2, m_1, q), there is an alternative technique T'' with parameters (m_2'', m_1'', q). The same type of machine, M_1, is used in producing C in the two techniques but they differ as to the type of

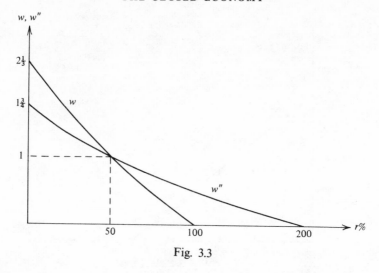

Fig. 3.3

basic machine used for producing M_1 and itself. Using an example again, suppose that for

$$T \text{ (as before)}; m_2 = 2, m_1 = 1, q = 7$$
$$T'' \qquad\qquad ; m_2'' = 3, m_1'' = 0.5, q = 7$$

On substituting into (4) one finds that

$$w = \left[\frac{7(1 - r)}{3 + r} \right], \qquad w'' = \left[\frac{7(2 - r)}{8 + 5r} \right]$$

These two wage–profit frontiers are shown in Fig. 3.3; they intersect only at $(w = w'' = 1, r = 50\%)$. It will be seen that T will be used for a wage greater than unity $(r < 50\%)$, while T'' will be chosen for a wage less than unity $(r > 50\%)$.

It should again be noted that one of two alternative techniques might completely dominate the other, making the latter economically irrelevant, and that the method of analysis can be extended to any number of alternative techniques. Indeed, this analysis need not be restricted to choices between techniques which differ only in one respect, as in this and the previous section, but can be applied to the choice between any techniques, however much they may differ. Thus suppose that there are two techniques T'', as above, and T''', where *both* the M_2 and the M_1 machine differ as between T'' and T'''. Let $m_2''' = m_1''' = 31/12, q''' = 31/13$. One can still draw the wage–profit frontiers on the same diagram, as in Fig. 3.4. (This example illustrates the possibility that two wage–profit frontiers may intersect

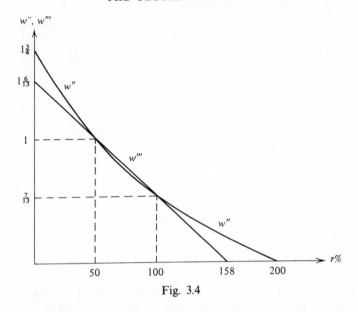

Fig. 3.4

twice for positive (r, w). This phenomenon, referred to as reswitching or double-switching, implies that a given technique may be used at both 'low' and 'high' profit rates (wage rates) and yet not be used at intermediate ones.)

Choice of technique and consumption output

Under competitive, capitalist conditions, that technique will be chosen which yields the highest profit rate (wage rate) for a given wage rate (profit rate). There is no reason why the chosen technique should be the one that yields the highest technically possible output of the consumption commodity, per unit of labour, for the relevant growth rate. Thus, suppose that there are two alternative techniques, with w/r and c/g frontiers as shown in Fig. 3.5, and that the real wage rate is exogenously fixed at $\bar{w}$. Clearly Technique 2 will be chosen, yielding a profit rate of $\bar{r}$.

Now if the capitalist's savings ratio, s, is relatively high, so that the growth rate $(g = s\bar{r})$ is equal to g_2, then the 'c' maximising technique will indeed be in use. But if s is relatively low, so that the growth rate is equal to g_1, then Technique 1 would give a higher value of 'c' for the growth rate g_1 but is not used. Analogously, if the growth rate were fixed exogenously, at say g_1, then with a 'high' value of s, the consumption maximising

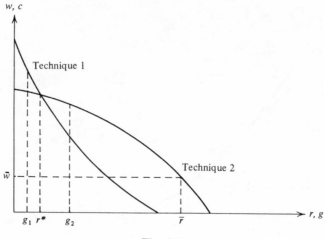

Fig. 3.5

Technique 1 will be used but for a 'low' value of s the profit rate ($r = g_1/s$) will exceed r^* and thus Technique 2 will be chosen, giving a lower 'c' than is technically possible at the growth rate g_1. In brief, competitive capitalist choice of technique may or may not be technically efficient, in the sense of maximising the consumption output per unit of labour consistent with the rate of growth. The only exception, when more than one technique is available, is in the case $g = r$, which, if workers do not save, entails that capitalists save all their profits.

More than one consumption commodity

Suppose now that there are several different types of consumption commodity; the principles involved in the analysis of such a situation may be brought out by assuming, at first, that there are just two consumption commodities, there being only one available technique for the production of each. It will be assumed, furthermore, that the M_2 type machine is the same for both techniques of production.

There are now two possibilities; either the M_1 machine is the same for each consumption commodity or it is not. If it is the same, then equation (4) applies to the second commodity, denoted by a dash, provided that w and q are replaced by w' and q'. It follows immediately that $(w/w') = (q/q')$. But (w/w'), the real wage in terms of the first consumption commodity divided by the real wage in terms of the second, is simply the value of the second consumption commodity in terms of the first, call it p'_c. Hence

$$p'_c = (q/q')$$

and p'_c is independent of income distribution.

If each consumption commodity is produced by its 'own' kind of M_1 machine, however, one finds from (4) that

$$(w/w') = p'_c = \left[\frac{m_1 q}{m'_1 q'}\right]\left[\frac{m'_1 m_2 + (m_2 - m'_1)(1 + r)}{m_1 m_2 + (m_2 - m_1)(1 + r)}\right] \qquad (19)$$

where the dashed variables again relate to the second consumption commodity. It follows from (19) that p'_c rises, remains constant or falls, as r rises (w and w' fall), according as $m_1 \gtreqless m'_1$. Thus, unless $m_1 = m'_1$, the relative values of the two consumption commodities depend on income distribution.

It will be clear that the above analysis may readily be extended to any number of consumption commodities. It can also be utilised in the analysis of systems in which there is a choice of technique. Thus suppose, to take a simple example, that there is only one technique for the production of the second consumption commodity but that there are two for the production of the first. The M_2 machine is common to all three techniques but each technique uses a different kind of M_1 machine. Suppose that for 'low' rates of profit, the technique for producing the first consumption commodity has $m_1 = m_1^* < m'_1$ but that for 'high' rates of profit the technique used has $m_1 = m_1^{**} > m'_1$. It then follows that p'_c will at first be falling as r rises but that subsequently p'_c will be rising as r rises. (Thus, when there is a choice of technique, the relative value of the consumption commodities need not be monotonically related to changes in income distribution.) The reader may consider more complex combinations of the number of consumption commodities and the number of alternative techniques for their production.

With more than one consumption commodity in the system, the pattern of labour allocations and physical outputs, for any growth rate, will depend on the pattern of consumption but an analysis of this question is not necessary for the purposes of the present work. Only in chapters 8 and 10 will a multiplicity of consumption commodities be considered again—and even then only under strong simplifying assumptions—since our principal focus of attention will be the produced means of production and their accumulation, rather than the role of consumption activities.

The analysis of trade

It is important that the reader should have mastered the above arguments, for they will be drawn on extensively in the following chapters on international trade. Most use will be made of the very simple case considered in part I of this chapter but in chapters 8 and 10 the complications introduced in part II will also be drawn on. It may be remarked that the introduction of such complications into our analysis of trade will not be found to modify greatly the conclusions reached in their absence; the simpler analyses should therefore not be belittled. It should also be noted, however, that the powerful assumptions of constant returns to scale, steady growth and strong competition will be retained throughout.

4
THE PATTERN OF TRADE FOR A SMALL ECONOMY

It is a well-established tradition in the theory of international trade that one should first analyse the properties of a single, 'small' open economy and then proceed to a more general analysis of international trade. The rationale of this procedure, which will be adopted here, is that the analysis of a single 'small' economy is relatively easy, is of interest in its own right and leads to conclusions which greatly facilitate a more complex analysis of trade which takes explicit account of all the economies involved.

The term 'small economy' does not refer, it should be noted, to the size of the economy as measured by, say, its population or national income: a small economy is one whose relative importance in world trade is sufficiently small that the economic actions of its capitalists and its government will have no effect on the relative prices at which commodities are exchanged on the world market. A small economy, in short, is one whose capitalists face *given* international prices; such an economy might be quite large in the everyday sense of that term.

In this chapter it will be shown how capitalists in a small, open economy will be led, by the profit motive, to adopt a certain pattern of production, exports and imports. In the next chapter the implications of trade for the relationship between the level of consumption and the rate of growth will be examined and in the following two the effects of government policy concerning tariffs, quotas, etc., will be considered. In chapter 8, the effects on the analysis of relaxing some of the simplifying assumptions—concerning the numbers of commodities, alternative production methods and the tradeability of commodities—will be examined. We shall then turn, in the last two chapters, to a multi-economy analysis of trade. It will be assumed throughout that both labour and money capital are internationally immobile.

THE METHOD OF ANALYSIS

The analysis presented in this and most of the subsequent chapters will take the form of comparative dynamics, i.e. of comparing the properties of two different, growing economies which are alike in many but not all respects. The two economies will be alike in that the same technical knowledge is available in each, that market conditions are strongly competitive, that the capitalists' savings ratio is the same in each and that either the growth rate or the wage rate is exogenously determined, at the same level, in each of the economies. Both economies will be assumed to be undergoing steady, equilibrium growth. The principal difference between the two economies will be that while one is an autarkic economy, the other is open to international trade. The 'effects' of trade will thus be found by showing how the two economies differ in other respects; thus a typical comparative dynamics question would be, 'At a common, exogenously given rate of steady growth, will the level of sustainable consumption per unit of labour be higher in the autarkic economy or in the open economy?'

It is important that the *comparative* nature of the analysis be fully recognised and that any temptation to interpret it as a covert analysis of the disequilibrium transition from autarky to trade be resisted. The analysis of transition from one steady growth path to another is not well-developed, even for a closed economy, and the method of comparative dynamics is thus the best that is ready to hand. Furthermore, while it may well be desirable to develop a disequilibrium analysis, it should not be assumed too readily that it would be more appropriate than comparative dynamics analysis for the particular purpose of showing the role of international trade. Our objective is to understand why trade is taking place between nations and what the consequences are; it is not to analyse the purely hypothetical process of opening autarkic economies to trade.

THE COMPETITIVE PRESSURE TO TRADE

Consider two economies of the type considered in part I of chapter 3; the same methods for the production of the three commodities C, M_1 and M_2, characterised by the parameters q, m_1 and m_2, are known and usable in each economy. One of the economies is autarkic, while the other is open to free trade at international prices, in terms of the consumption commodity, of P_1 and P_2 for commodities M_1 and M_2 respectively. The left-hand column of Table 4.1 shows the relations between the wage rate, the profit rate and prices that must hold in the autarkic economy; they are simply equations (1), (2) and (3) of chapter 3. The right-hand column shows the corresponding relation for each industry which will obtain, in the open economy, *if* that industry exists. While all three relations in the

Table 4.1

	Autarky	Free trade
C industry	$w + p_1(1 + r) = q$	$w + P_1(1 + r) = q$
M_1 industry	$w + p_2(1 + r) = m_1 p_1$	$w + P_2(1 + r) = m_1 P_1$
M_2 industry	$w + p_2(1 + r) = m_2 p_2$	$w + P_2(1 + r) = m_2 P_2$

autarky column must hold simultaneously, given that C is being produced, there is no presumption that all three relations in the free trade column must hold, for each equation there applies only when its industry actually exists in the open economy. Since either one or two of the three industries may not exist in the open economy, the commodities not produced domestically being imported in exchange for exports of the commodity or commodities produced, it follows that the equations in the right-hand column are to be regarded as alternatives, not as relations that hold simultaneously. (More formally, each equality in the right-hand column could be written as a weak inequality, $\geq$, with the implication that the strict equality holds if and only if the industry in question either exists or is on the margin of operation. The presentation adopted in Table 4.1 will, however, perhaps be easier to follow for some readers.)

Suppose now that the wage rate is given exogenously, in both the autarkic and the open economy, at the level $w = \bar{w}$. Suppose that $P_1 < p_1$ and consider the first row of Table 4.1; it is clear that the rate of profit will be higher in the free trade column than in the autarky column. It follows that, at $w = \bar{w}$ and $P_1 < p_1$, capitalists in the open economy could, by specialising in the production of commodity C, obtain a higher profit rate than their autarky counterparts. Suppose now that $P_1 > p_1, P_2 < p_2$ and consider the second row of Table 4.1; it follows that specialisation in the production of M_1 will yield a higher profit rate than obtains in the autarkic economy. Finally, let $P_2 > p_2$ and consider the third row of Table 4.1; specialisation in the production of M_2 will clearly yield a rate of profit higher than the autarky profit rate. But we have now shown that at *any* (P_1, P_2) different from (p_1, p_2), there is at least one specialisation yielding a rate of profit higher than the autarky one.

If, by contrast, it were assumed that the two economies had the same exogenously given growth rate and hence profit rate, $r = \bar{r}$, it could be shown, in just the same way, that at any (P_1, P_2) different from (p_1, p_2) there is at least one free trade specialisation yielding a real wage rate greater than the autarky wage rate. It may be concluded that, subject to one qualification, under competitive conditions capitalists who can engage in free trade will be driven actually to do so by the pressure of competition.

The qualification just referred to is that (P_1, P_2) might *equal* (p_1, p_2); in this (certainly marginal) case, competition would not lead capitalists to specialise or not to specialise but would leave them indifferent between autarky, specialisation in any industry, or semi-specialisation in any two industries.

THE CHOICE OF SPECIALISATION

The argument of the previous section showed that, under competitive conditions, capitalists in a small, open economy will be led to engage in trade, since trade is 'profitable'. It did not, however, show which pattern of production and trade will be adopted, i.e. which pattern is the 'most profitable', at any given (P_1, P_2).

Modifying the argument used in the previous section, it can be seen from the first row of Table 4.1 that if $P_1 > p_1$ then specialisation in C will *not* be adopted and from the third row that if $P_2 < p_2$ then specialisation in M_2 will *not* be adopted. Now consider the second and third rows of the free trade column; it will be clear that if $m_1P_1 < m_2P_2$ then an M_1 specialisation will *not* be adopted since an M_2 specialisation would be more profitable, while if $m_1P_1 > m_2P_2$ the position is exactly reversed. Putting these four negative rules together, one may draw Fig. 4.1, in which the set of all non-negative (P_1, P_2) is divided up into five regions. In the region marked C, the four negative rules alone suffice to show that

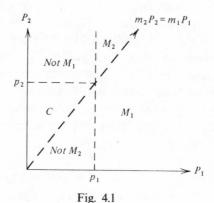

Fig. 4.1

a C specialisation will be the most profitable for any (P_1, P_2) lying in that region; analogous remarks apply to the regions marked M_1 and M_2. In the remaining two regions, the four negative rules only suffice to rule out one of the possible specialisations. The reader is invited to check that Fig. 4.1 can indeed be derived from the four negative rules and that those rules apply whether the wage rate or the profit rate is regarded as exogenously determined.

FURTHER ANALYSIS OF THE CHOICE OF SPECIALISATION

We must now show which specialisation will be chosen for international prices (P_1, P_2) which fall in the region marked '$Not\ M_1$' or in that marked '$Not\ M_2$' in Fig. 4.1. Consider the former region; clearly the most profitable specialisation must be in C or in M_2, unless (P_1, P_2) are such that the C and the M_2 specialisations are equally profitable. It will therefore be helpful to see whether there exist combinations of P_1 and P_2 which make the C and M_2 specialisations equally profitable, just as the line separating the M_1 and M_2 regions, in Fig. 4.1, consists of (P_1, P_2) lying on $m_2 P_2 = m_1 P_1$, implying that M_1 and M_2 specialisations are equally profitable.

At this point in the analysis it does, unfortunately, matter whether the wage rate or the profit rate is regarded as exogenously determined. It will first be assumed that the profit rate is exogenously determined at $r = \bar{r}$; it is shown below that the analysis is very similar with a given wage rate. It will be seen from Table 4.1 that, with $r = \bar{r}$, the real wage implied by a C specialisation is given by $w = [q - (1 + \bar{r})P_1]$, while that implied by an M_2 specialisation is given by $w = P_2[m_2 - (1 + \bar{r})]$. Thus either specialisation will yield the same real wage, with $r = \bar{r}$, whenever

$$P_2 = \left[\frac{q - (1 + \bar{r})P_1}{m_2 - (1 + \bar{r})} \right] \tag{1}$$

(1) is the equation of a downward sloping straight line which passes through the point $P_1 = p_1, P_2 = p_2$. Thus if the segment of the graph of (1) which lies 'north-west' of (p_1, p_2) is drawn in Fig. 4.1, the '$Not\ M_1$' region will be divided into a C region and an M_2 region, a C specialisation yielding the highest real wage for (P_1, P_2) lying below the line and an M_2 specialisation doing the same for (P_1, P_2) lying above the line.

The '$Not\ M_2$' region in Fig. 4.1 can be divided in the same way. From Table 4.1, the real wage with a C specialisation is, for $r = \bar{r}$, given by $w = [q - (1 + \bar{r})P_1]$, while that for an M_1 specialisation is given by w

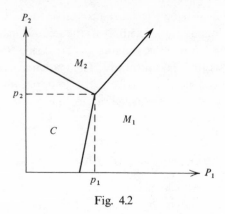

Fig. 4.2

$= [m_1 P_1 - (1 + \bar{r}) P_2]$. Thus the real wage will be the same with either specialisation when

$$P_2 = \left[\frac{-q + (m_1 + 1 + \bar{r}) P_1}{1 + \bar{r}} \right] \tag{2}$$

(2) is the equation of an upward sloping straight line, which passes through (p_1, p_2). Thus drawing the graph of (2) to the 'south-west' of (p_1, p_2), in Fig. 4.1, the 'Not M_2' region is divided into a C and an M_1 region, a C specialisation being adopted to the left of the line and an M_1 specialisation being adopted to the right. With both the 'Not M_1' and the 'Not M_2' regions divided in this way, Fig. 4.1 becomes Fig. 4.2.

THE PROXIMATE DETERMINANTS OF SPECIALISATION

Consider Fig. 4.2, bearing in mind that the lines separating the three regions, which we may call 'the lines of semi-specialisation', depend upon the given values of q, m_1, m_2 and $\bar{r}$. It is clear from Fig. 4.2 that, for given technical conditions and rate of profit, the choice of specialisation is determined by the given international prices (P_1, P_2). Provided that (P_1, P_2) fall unambiguously within one of the three regions C, M_1, M_2 of Fig. 4.2, the forces of competition will lead capitalists to specialise completely in the production of a single commodity. If, however, (P_1, P_2) should lie on one of the lines of semi-specialisation, then competitive forces will lead capitalists to produce either or both of the appropriate commodities and specialisation may or may not be complete. Finally, of course, if international prices should be identical to the autarky prices corresponding to the profit rate $\bar{r}$, then the with-trade real wage will equal the autarky real wage whether capitalists produce any one, any two or all three of the commodities, so that the pattern of 'specialisation' will be indeterminate.

It is now necessary to show how, for given international prices (P_1, P_2), the choice of specialisation depends on technical conditions and on the rate of profit. Taking the technical conditions first, consider, in addition to the autarkic and the open economies compared so far, a third economy. This third economy is a small, open one, facing the given international prices (P_1, P_2) and having the same rate of profit, $\bar{r}$, as the other two economies. The technical conditions in the third economy may be taken to be identical to those in the other economies with respect to two of the industries but different with respect to the remaining industry. One can now ask how the given difference in technical conditions will affect the choice of specialisation.

In Fig. 4.3(a), the solid lines are the lines of semi-specialisation for the first open economy. The dashed lines, together with that part of the M_1M_2 line of semi-specialisation which lies to the 'north-east' of their intersection, are the lines of semi-specialisation for the second open economy, which is like the first in all respects, apart from having a higher value of q. The regions marked C, M_1 and M_2 are common to both economies but those marked C^+, while belonging to the region of C specialisation for the second economy, belong to the M_1 or M_2 regions for the first. Thus the set of international prices (P_1, P_2) which will induce capitalists to specialise in the production of C is, other things being equal, larger for the economy which is more efficient in the production of C, i.e. for the second economy with the higher value of q.

Interpreting Figs. 4.3(b) and (c) analogously, it will be seen that, other things being equal, the set of international prices inducing a specialisation

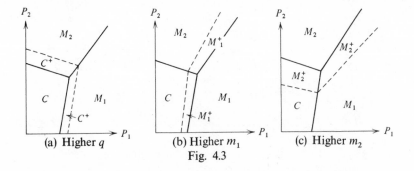

(a) Higher q (b) Higher m_1 (c) Higher m_2

Fig. 4.3

in M_1 is larger for an economy which is more efficient in the production of M_1 (Fig. 4.3(b)), while a larger set of international prices will induce an M_2 specialisation for an economy more efficient in the production of M_2 (Fig. 4.3(c)).

It clearly follows from the above discussion of Figs. 4.3 that, for a given rate of profit and given international prices, the pattern of specialisation depends on technical conditions of production in the small, open economy.

In order to see how the given rate of profit, $\bar{r}$, influences the choice of specialisation, consider now two small, open economies which are alike in all respects, other than in having different exogenously given rates of profit, say $\bar{r}$ and $\hat{r}$. (This difference in rates of profit might be the result of differences in the growth rates and/or the savings behaviour of capitalists in the two economies, it should be recalled.) It is necessary to consider the three possible cases $m_1 \gtreqless m_2$, so let us take first the simplest case, $m_1 = m_2 = m$ say, shown in Fig. 4.4(b). In this case, prices in an autarkic economy are independent of the rate of profit, being given by $p_1 = p_2 = (q/m)$. In Fig. 4.4(b) the solid lines are the lines of semi-specialisation for the economy with the lower rate of profit, say $\bar{r}$, while the broken lines, together with the M_1M_2 line of semi-specialisation, are those for the economy with the higher rate, say $\hat{r}$. (The fact that the point of intersection of the lines of semi-specialisation is the same for both economies reflects, of course, the result that autarky prices are independent of the rate of profit when $m_1 = m_2$.) If international prices, (P_1, P_2), should fall in one of the regions marked C, M_1 or M_2 in Fig. 4.4(b), then the pattern of specialisation will be the same in both economies. If, however, international prices should fall in either of the shaded regions in Fig. 4.4(b), then the pattern of specialisa-

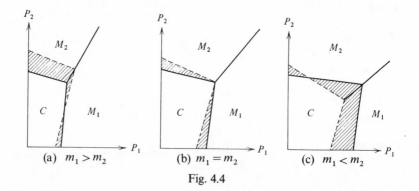

(a) $m_1 > m_2$ (b) $m_1 = m_2$ (c) $m_1 < m_2$

Fig. 4.4

tion will differ as between the two economies, as a result of the difference in their given rates of profit.

Figs. 4.4(a) and (c), for the cases $m_1 \neq m_2$, are to be interpreted in much the same way as Fig. 4.4(b); it remains true that the $M_1 M_2$ line of semi-specialisation is the same for both economies but that the CM_1 and CM_2 lines of semi-specialisation differ as between the two economies due to their having different rates of profit. The only complication arising from the non-equality of m_1 and m_2 is that autarky prices now depend on the given rate of profit and that, as a result, the point of intersection of the lines of semi-specialisation differs as between the two economies. As a consequence of this, in each of Figs. 4.4(a) and (c) there are *three* regions such that, if international prices should fall therein, the pattern of specialisation will differ as between the two economies, simply because they have different rates of profit. (In the regions marked C, M_1 or M_2 the difference in profit rates will not lead to any difference in specialisation.)

Drawing the above findings together, it may be concluded that the pattern of specialisation—or semi-specialisation—in a small, open economy, with an exogenously given rate of profit, will be determined by the pattern of international prices, the technical conditions of production in that economy and the level of the given rate of profit. Of course, these proximate determinants of the pattern of specialisation may themselves be open to further explanation.

A MODIFICATION TO THE ABOVE ANALYSIS

It will be recalled that the derivation of Fig. 4.1 was independent of whether the wage rate or the profit rate was held constant but that the division of the regions 'Not M_1' and 'Not M_2' given above had to be based on the assumption of a given rate of profit. It must now be shown that the analysis is little altered if one assumes, by contrast, that the wage rate is exogenously determined at, say, the level $w = \bar{w}$.

From the first and third entries in the free trade column of Table 4.1, it will be seen that, with $w = \bar{w}$, a C specialisation and an M_2 specialisation will yield the same rate of profit whenever

$$P_2 = \left[\frac{\bar{w}P_1}{m_2 P_1 - (q - \bar{w})} \right] \tag{3}$$

In the same way, from the first and second entries, it will be seen that a C specialisation and an M_1 specialisation will yield the same rate of

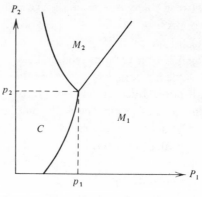

Fig. 4.5

profit if

$$P_2 = \left[\frac{(m_1 P_1 - \bar{w})P_1}{q - \bar{w}} \right] \tag{4}$$

(3) is the equation of a negatively inclined rectangular hyperbola, while (4) is the equation of a parabola, the economically relevant part of which is upward sloping; both curves necessarily pass through the point (p_1, p_2). Thus when the relevant parts of curves (3) and (4) are drawn in, Fig. 4.1 becomes Fig. 4.5. Fig. 4.5 is essentially the same as Fig. 4.2, which applied when the rate of profit was held constant, but the CM_1 and CM_2 lines of semi-specialisation are now curves instead of straight lines and the CM_2 line no longer intersects the P_2 axis.

It will be left to the reader to check that, using Fig. 4.5 in place of Fig. 4.2, the analysis of the previous section can be repeated to show that, for a small, open economy with a given wage rate, the pattern of specialisation —or semi-specialisation—will be proximately determined by the pattern of international prices, the technical conditions of production in that economy and the level of the given wage rate.

It may be noted that the pattern of specialisation, induced by given international prices, may depend on whether it is the wage rate or the profit rate that is exogenously determined. Consider three economies with identical technical conditions. Let one of them be autarkic, with wage and profit rates $\bar{w}$ and $\bar{r}$; let the other two be small, open economies, one of them with an exogenously determined wage rate $\bar{w}$ and the other with an exogenously determined rate of profit, $\bar{r}$. In Fig. 4.6, which is drawn for the

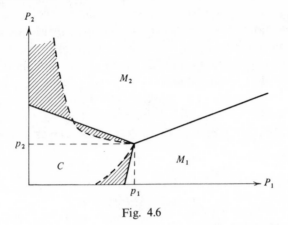

Fig. 4.6

case $m_1 < m_2$, the solid lines of semi-specialisation are those for the open economy with a given rate of profit, while the broken ones are those for the open economy with a given wage rate; the $M_1 M_2$ line of semi-specialisation applies to both, of course. Now if the international prices (P_1, P_2) should fall in one of the regions marked C, M_1 or M_2 in Fig. 4.6, then the pattern of specialisation will be the same in both open economies. If international prices should lie in one of the three shaded regions of Fig. 4.6, however, those given prices will induce different specialisations in the two economies, the implication being that, at such prices, the specialisation that maximises the profit rate, given $\bar{w}$, is not the specialisation that maximises the wage rate, given $\bar{r}$. This point will be further discussed in the next section.

AN ALTERNATIVE TECHNIQUE OF ANALYSIS

In the technique of analysis used above—dividing the set of non-negative international prices into three regions of specialisation—attention was drawn explicitly to the role of international prices but the role of the given wage or profit rate was left somewhat implicit. It may therefore be helpful to introduce an alternative method of analysis, which makes explicit the role of the distributive variables. While this alternative analysis will produce no new results in the present chapter, it will prove useful subsequently.

Let us again consider two economies with the same available methods of production, one an autarkic economy, with wage rate, profit rate and prices $\bar{w}, \bar{r}, p_1$ and p_2 respectively, and the other a small, open economy, facing international prices P_1 and P_2 and having either a given wage rate, $\bar{w}$, or a given rate of profit, $\bar{r}$. It will be convenient to consider the case $m_1 > m_2$, leaving the reader to effect the necessary modifications to the argument for the cases $m_1 \leqq m_2$. Fig. 4.7 shows the wage–profit frontier for the autarkic economy; it should be noted carefully that the frontier has been extended to the (notional) point $r = -1, w = q$. Now consider the entries in the free trade column of Table 4.1, rewritten as follows:

$$w = q - P_1(1 + r) \tag{5}$$
$$w = m_1 P_1 - P_2(1 + r) \tag{6}$$
$$w = m_2 P_2 - P_2(1 + r) \tag{7}$$

Since international prices (P_1, P_2) are given, each of (5), (6) and (7) gives a downward sloping, linear wage–profit frontier, holding when the corresponding specialisation is adopted. It will be seen that (5) always passes through the point $r = -1, w = q$, that (7) always passes through the point $r = (m_2 - 1), w = 0$ and that (6) is always parallel to (7), lying above or below (7) according as $m_1 P_1 \gtrless m_2 P_2$. Now suppose that $P_1 = p_1$ and $P_2 = p_2$; (5), (6) and (7) will then be the three relations which hold simultaneously in the autarkic economy and therefore each of them will necessarily pass through the point $(\bar{r}, \bar{w})$. Thus the straight lines marked C, M_1 and M_2 in Fig. 4.7 are the lines (5), (6) and (7) for the case $P_1 = p_1, P_2 = p_2$—note that, in this case, lines (6) and (7) coincide, since $m_1 p_1 = m_2 p_2$.

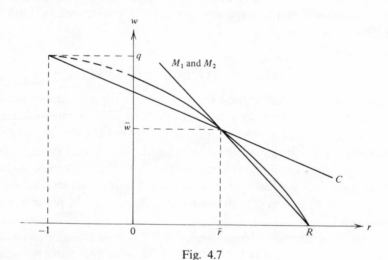

Fig. 4.7

The four 'negative rules' discussed above are now readily established within the present framework. Thus if $P_1 > p_1$, the line (5) will have a steeper slope than the line marked C in Fig. 4.7; it will therefore pass below the point $(\bar{r}, \bar{w})$ and thus a C specialisation will never be adopted if $P_1 > p_1$. Again, if $P_2 < p_2$, the line (7) will pass below $(\bar{r}, \bar{w})$ and hence an M_2 specialisation will never be adopted in such circumstances. Finally, if $m_1 P_1 > m_2 P_2$, line (6) will lie above line (7), so that an M_2 specialisation will not be adopted, while if $m_1 P_1 < m_2 P_2$, an M_1 specialisation will not be adopted. As was pointed out above, these negative rules suffice to determine the chosen specialisation for given international prices, except when $P_1 < p_1, P_2 > p_2$—in which case an M_1 specialisation will not be chosen—and when $P_1 < p_1, m_2 P_2 > m_1 P_1$— in which case an M_2 specialisation will not be adopted. To see how the latter cases may be analysed using the present technique, consider, for example, the case $P_1 < p_1, P_2 > p_2$. As is shown in Fig. 4.8, lines (5) and (7) both pass above the point $(\bar{r}, \bar{w})$. In Fig. 4.8(a), P_1 is significantly less than p_1, while P_2 is little greater than p_2, with the result that, at these international prices, a C specialisation will be chosen whether it is the wage rate, $\bar{w}$, or the rate of profit, $\bar{r}$, which is exogenously determined in the open economy. In Fig. 4.8(c), the position is the reverse of that in Fig. 4.8(a), with the wage–profit frontier for an M_2 specialisation dominating the C specialisation frontier both at $w = \bar{w}$ and at $r = \bar{r}$.

In Fig. 4.8(b), however, a C specialisation will maximise the rate of profit for $w = \bar{w}$, while an M_2 specialisation will maximise the real wage rate for $r = \bar{r}$, thus illustrating the result, obtained above, that the specialisation chosen at given international prices may depend on whether it is the wage rate or the profit rate that is given exogenously. (The CM_2 lines of semi-specialisation in Figs. 4.2 and 4.5 are, of course, those sets of international prices (P_1, P_2) which cause the C and M_2 lines in Fig. 4.8 to coincide at $r = \bar{r}$ or at $w = \bar{w}$, respectively.)

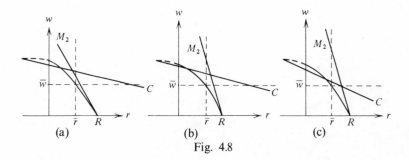

Fig. 4.8

SUMMARY

It has been seen that, under conditions of free trade, competitive forces will lead capitalists in a small, open economy to adopt a pattern of specialisation (or semi-specialisation) for any international relative prices not equal to autarky relative prices. The *proximate* determinants of the pattern of specialisation (or semi-specialisation) will be (i) the set of international relative prices (ii) the technical characteristics of the methods of production available in the economy and (iii) the level of the exogenously given real wage rate or rate of profit. *Ceteris paribus*, the more efficient is the production of a given commodity, the larger is the set of international relative prices which will induce a specialisation in the production and export of that commodity. It was noted that, for given international prices and given conditions of production, the specialisation which maximises the rate of profit (for an exogenously given real wage rate) may or may not be the specialisation which maximises the real wage rate (for an exogenously given rate of profit).

5

THE GAIN FROM TRADE
IN A SMALL ECONOMY

Having seen how the pattern of trade is determined, we may now turn to the traditional question whether a country necessarily 'gains from trade', whether, that is, the consumption possibilities open to a trading economy are necessarily superior to those available to an otherwise similar autarkic economy. This question is often discussed in terms of stationary economies with two different consumption commodities—and it will indeed be discussed in those terms in chapter 8—but in this chapter the criterion of gain will be whether a superior combination of consumption level and rate of growth is possible with trade; the precise interpretation to be given to this criterion will emerge below.

It may be helpful to dismiss from the outset the superficial argument that 'Countries must gain from free trade, for if they did not, they would choose to be autarkic'. The fallacy in this argument lies in the fact that 'countries' do not, in the relevant sense, choose to trade or not to trade. Under free trade, decisions are made by individual capitalists, under the pressures of competition, and the resultant effects on the 'country', whether beneficial or harmful, are unforeseen and unintended consequences of those decisions. Thus the question whether countries gain from trade is left open.

In chapter 3, it was noted that, when there is a choice of technique, there is no guarantee that the technique chosen by capitalists in a closed economy will yield the highest possible level of consumption, per unit of labour, unless the growth rate of the economy is equal to the rate of profit. Now the decision to adopt a particular specialisation, in an open economy, may be regarded as a choice of technique on the part of the capitalists. Thus, if the implied analogy holds good, the presumption must be that, when the rate of growth is less than the rate of profit, the gain from trade may be positive or it may be negative. It will be seen below that this presumption is justified.

It must be remembered throughout this chapter that the method of analysis is that of comparative dynamics, a *comparison* being made between two economies with identical technical knowledge and capitalists' savings ratios, s. One of the economies is autarkic, with rates of wages, profits and growth given by $\bar{w}, \bar{r}$ and $\bar{g} = s\bar{r}$ respectively, while the other is a small, open economy, with either given rates of profit and growth, $\bar{r}$ and $\bar{g}$ (where $\bar{g} = s\bar{r}$), or a given wage rate, $\bar{w}$. No study will be attempted of any possible path of transition from autarky to trade, or *vice versa*. (It may be remarked, in passing, that to be of any significance such a study would have to take full account of the existence of durable fixed capital and of the possible need to scrap many partially worn machines in the course of the transitional process. The assumptions of steady growth and of a uniform rate of profit would, of course, have to be dropped.)

The analysis will be presented in full for the case of given $\bar{r}$ and $\bar{g}$, with one section devoted to indicating how the analysis can be modified for the case of given $\bar{w}$.

THE CONSUMPTION–GROWTH FRONTIER FOR AN OPEN ECONOMY

The exports from and imports into a real world economy do not need to be balanced, even with a fixed exchange rate; foreign exchange reserves may accumulate and there may be net flows of international investment and international payments of interest and profit. Yet since the examination of international investment and monetary phenomena lies beyond the scope of this work, it will be appropriate to assume balanced trade, leaving to others the task of modifying the analysis when that assumption is relaxed.

Suppose first that international prices are such as to induce a C specialisation and consider the flows of commodities involved, per unit of employment. Output of the consumption commodity will be q, so that if domestic consumption is c, then exports, per unit of employment, will be $(q - c)$. These exports will have to pay for the required imports of M_1 machines, namely $(1 + g)$ machines, with a value of $P_1(1 + g)$. Hence, when trade is balanced,

$$(q - c) = P_1(1 + g)$$

or

$$c = q - P_1(1 + g) \tag{1}$$

The values of q and P_1 being given, (1), the equation of a downward sloping straight line, is the with-trade consumption–growth frontier. As was seen in chapter 4, with a C specialisation the wage–profit frontier is given by

$$w = q - P_1(1 + r),$$

so that the consumption–growth frontier and the wage–profit frontier are identical, just as in the closed economy. It will be noted that, other things being equal, the consumption–growth frontier (1) is unambiguously higher, the higher is q—i.e. the more efficient is the C industry—and the lower is P_1, i.e. the less consumption commodity has to be exchanged on the world market for each M_1 machine imported.

Now suppose instead that international prices lead capitalists to adopt an M_1 specialisation, M_1 machines being produced and exported, while M_2 machines and C are imported. Reckoning all physical quantities per unit of employment, as above, output and exports of M_1 machines will be m_1, with value $m_1 P_1$. The value of imports, on the other hand, will be $P_2(1 + g)$ for M_2 machines plus c for the consumption commodity. Hence, with balanced trade,

$$m_1 P_1 = P_2(1 + g) + c$$

or

$$c = m_1 P_1 - P_2(1 + g) \qquad (2)$$

With given values for m_1, P_1 and P_2, (2) is the equation of a negatively inclined, linear consumption–growth frontier. It is simply the wage–profit frontier for an M_1 specialisation, with w replaced by c and r replaced by g. It will be seen that, other things being equal, the consumption–growth frontier (2) is unambiguously higher, the higher is m_1 (the more efficient is the M_1 industry), the higher is P_1 (the consumption value of exported machines) and the lower is P_2 (the consumption value of imported machines).

Finally, suppose that international prices induce an M_2 specialisation, with M_2 machines being produced and exported, while C is imported. Per unit of employment, output of M_2 machines will be m_2 but $(1 + g)$ of these will be used domestically, so that exports of M_2 machines will be $[m_2 - (1 + g)]$, with value $P_2[m_2 - (1 + g)]$. Since imports will simply be c, it follows that, with balanced trade,

$$c = m_2 P_2 - P_2(1 + g) \qquad (3)$$

We again have a linear, downward sloping consumption–growth frontier, which is identical to the corresponding wage–profit frontier. Other things

being equal, the consumption–growth frontier (3) is unambiguously higher, the higher is m_2 (efficiency in the M_2 export industry) and the higher is P_2 (the consumption value of the export).

THE CONSUMPTION-OPTIMAL SPECIALISATION

In deriving (1), (2) and (3) it was immaterial whether the wage rate or the rate of profit was exogenously given; it was enough to assume that a certain specialisation was adopted at the given international prices. To proceed further, however, we shall, until the contrary is stated, assume that the rates of growth and profit, $\bar{g} = s\bar{r}$, are given.

With g given as $\bar{g}$, each of (1), (2) and (3) shows how c depends on international prices and the pattern of specialisation. Now, just as in chapter 4 it was shown that certain international prices yield the same real wage, for a given $\bar{r}$, whichever of two specialisations is adopted, so it can be seen from (1), (2) and (3) that, with $g = \bar{g}$, certain international prices will yield the same value of c whichever of two specialisations is chosen. Indeed, since (1), (2) and (3) are simply the wage–profit frontiers of chapter 4, with c in place of w and $\bar{g}$ in place of $\bar{r}$, this analysis has, in effect, already been carried out in chapter 4. The lines of semi-specialisation obtained in that chapter are, with $\bar{r}$ replaced by $\bar{g}$, the sets of international prices at which two different specialisations yield the same c, $\bar{g}$ being given. Thus Fig. 5.1 simply reproduces Fig. 4.2, the interpretation now being, however, that the label attached to each region shows the specialisation which, for international prices falling in that region, will maximise the value of c for the given growth rate. (Note that the three dividing lines in Fig. 5.1 do not

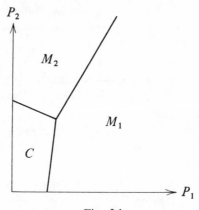

Fig. 5.1

meet at $P_1 = p_1, P_2 = p_2$, unless $\bar{g} = \bar{r}$, i.e. capitalists save and reinvest all their profits, *or* $m_1 = m_2$.)

THE CONSUMPTION OPTIMALITY OF TRADE

Suppose now that $\bar{g} < \bar{r}$ and consider Fig. 5.2, in which the broken lines are the lines of semi-specialisation and the solid lines are the lines which, as in Fig. 5.1, divide the set of non-negative international prices into regions showing the specialisation which is best for consumption, given $\bar{g}$. (Note that Fig. 5.2 simply reproduces Fig. 4.4, only the interpretation being different.) In Fig. 5.2, if international prices fall in one of the regions marked C, M_1 or M_2, then the pressure of competitive forces will indeed lead capitalists to adopt the specialisation which yields the greatest consumption, per unit of employment, which is possible with the given growth rate. If, however, international prices should fall in one of the shaded regions in Fig. 5.2, then capitalists will choose a specialisation which is non-optimal in terms of consumption. For example, if international prices, (P_1, P_2), lie in the 'north-westerly' shaded region of Fig. 5.2(a), then capitalists will adopt a C specialisation, although an M_2 specialisation would give a higher value of c with, by assumption, the same value of $g(=\bar{g})$. It may be noted that, when $m_1 \geq m_2$, a capitalist choice of the M_2 specialisation will necessarily be optimal for consumption (while a C or an M_1 specialisation may or may not be) but that, when $m_1 < m_2$, each of the three specialisations may or may not be optimal for consumption.

Fig. 5.2 is drawn on the assumption that $\bar{g} < \bar{r}$, i.e. that the capitalists' savings ratio, s, is less than unity. In the limiting case $s = 1$, of course, $\bar{g} = \bar{r}$ and the broken lines in Fig. 5.2 coincide with the corresponding solid

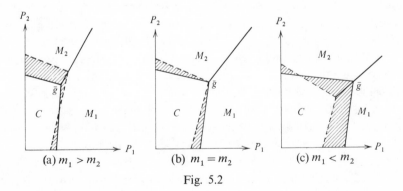

Fig. 5.2

lines, so that the shaded areas vanish. Thus when $\bar{g} = \bar{r}$, the capitalist choice of specialisation is necessarily optimal in terms of consumption, just as, with $g = r$, the capitalist choice of technique in an autarkic economy is necessarily optimal in the same sense. As we notionally decrease s from unity, holding $\bar{g}$ fixed and letting $r(= \bar{g}/s)$ increase to its maximum value of $(m_2 - 1)$, the shaded areas in Fig. 5.2 expand and thus the set of international prices at which specialisation will be non-optimal also expands. Speaking rather loosely, one might say that the adopted specialisation is 'more likely' to be non-optimal for consumption, the smaller is the capitalists' savings ratio.

THE GAIN FROM TRADE

While it has been shown in the last section that, with $\bar{g} < \bar{r}$, the choice of specialisation may be 'non-optimal' for consumption, it does not follow immediately that the with-trade level of consumption, per unit of employment, can be inferior to the autarky level and it is the comparison between the trade and autarky situations that is referred to when one speaks of the 'gain from trade'. It must now be considered whether with-trade consumption, even if non-optimal, is necessarily superior to autarky consumption, i.e. whether the gain from trade is necessarily positive.

Suppose first that international prices should be equal to the prices that would obtain in an autarkic economy with a *profit* rate of $\bar{g}$; these are the prices at point $\bar{g}$ in Fig. 5.2. (Only in the case $m_1 = m_2$ do these prices equal p_1, p_2.) In this case, the with-trade level of consumption would be exactly equal to the autarky level of consumption, given $\bar{g}$, whichever specialisation the capitalists might adopt. (This is shown in Fig. 5.2 by the fact that $\bar{g}$ is the intersection of the three solid lines.) This very special case aside, however, at any other set of international prices there is a specialisation yielding a with-trade consumption level which exceeds the corresponding autarky level. It follows immediately that when the chosen specialisation is optimal for consumption, the gain from trade is positive.

Suppose now, however, that international prices induce a 'non-optimal' specialisation. An example, for the case $m_1 > m_2$, will suffice to show that the gain from trade may be positive, zero or negative; readers are encouraged to consolidate their grasp of the technique of analysis used by examining other examples. In Fig. 5.2(a), let $P_2 = p_2$ and consider alternative values of P_1 between p_1 and zero. It will be clear that for P_1 just marginally smaller than p_1, a C specialisation will be adopted, although an

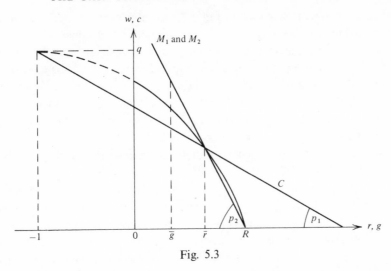

Fig. 5.3

M_2 specialisation would be optimal for consumption. To see that the level of consumption achieved may actually fall short of the autarky level, so that the gain from trade is negative, it will be useful to turn to the alternative method of analysis introduced at the end of chapter 4.

Consider Fig. 5.3, in which the with-trade wage–profit (consumption–growth) frontiers which would obtain when $P_1 = p_1, P_2 = p_2$, are marked as C, M_1 and M_2—cf. Fig. 4.7. Suppose now that $P_2 = p_2$ but $P_1 = (p_1 - \bar{p})$, where $\bar{p}$ is positive but very small. The frontier for an M_2 specialisation will still be as shown in Fig. 5.3, being $w = [m_2 p_2 - p_2(1 + r)]$, but that for an M_1 specialisation will lie lower than shown in Fig. 5.3, having shifted from $w = [m_1 p_1 - p_2(1 + r)]$ to $w = [m_1(p_1 - \bar{p}) - p_2(1 + r)]$. The frontier for a C specialisation, $w = [q - (p_1 - \bar{p})(1 + r)]$, will still pass through the point $(r = -1, w = q)$ but will otherwise lie above the frontier marked C in Fig. 5.3. It follows that a C specialisation will be adopted, for that choice maximises the real wage at profit rate $\bar{r}$, but that an M_2 specialisation would maximise c, consumption per unit of employment, at $\bar{g}$; these two results merely confirm what was said in the previous paragraph concerning Fig. 5.2(a). It is clear from Fig. 5.3, however, that more can be said, namely that, for sufficiently small $\bar{p}$, the frontier for the C specialisation, while being higher than the autarky frontier at $\bar{r}$, will be lower than the autarky frontier at $\bar{g}$. Hence capitalists will choose a specialisation which implies a *negative* 'gain from trade'.

As we notionally increase $\bar{p}$, i.e. decrease P_1, the frontier for a C

specialisation will 'swing up' in Fig. 5.3, until the level of c, at $\bar{g}$, is exactly equal to the autarky level. Continuing the notional decrease of P_1, with $P_2 = p_2$, the gain from trade becomes positive and, indeed, when P_1 is reduced sufficiently the C specialisation becomes optimal for consumption at $\bar{g}$. (In Fig. 5.2(a), by contrast, the C specialisation is still non-optimal for consumption even when $P_1 = 0$. The two figures are not inconsistent however; the C specialisation does or does not become optimal as P_1 falls to zero according as $(s + \bar{g})m_2 \gtrless (1 - s)\bar{g}m_1$.)

It may be concluded that in a small, open economy, with given but different rates of profit and growth, the specialisation chosen by capitalists, under the pressure of competition, may be optimal for consumption, non-optimal but yielding a positive gain from trade or such as to yield an actual 'loss from trade'. Speaking somewhat loosely, perhaps, one may say that non-optimality and loss from trade are 'more likely' the greater is the divergence between the rates of profit and growth, i.e. the smaller is the capitalists' savings ratio, s.

TRADE, CONSUMPTION AND GROWTH WITH A GIVEN WAGE

Suppose now that the small, open economy has the same exogenously given wage, $\bar{w}$, as the autarkic economy with which it is compared, rather than having the same rates of profit and growth, as assumed above. At any international prices not equal to the autarky prices, (p_1, p_2), the rate of profit will be greater in the open economy than in the autarkic one. Since we assume that $g = sr$ in both economies, it follows that, in general, the growth rate, g, will differ as between the two economies. But the level of consumption, c, will also generally differ as between the two economies, so that, with both c and g different, we seem to have no firm basis of comparison for assessing the gain from trade. However, before confronting this problem head on, it may be useful to consider the two special cases in which it does not arise.

Suppose, first, that the capitalists' savings ratio is unity, so that $g = r$ and $c = \bar{w}$ in both the open and the autarkic economy. Since the level of consumption is the same in both economies, while the rate of growth (equal to the rate of profit) will be higher in the open one, it may be said unambiguously that there is a positive gain from trade. On the other hand, if the capitalists' savings ratio should be zero, then the rate of growth will be zero in both economies and there is again a common basis for comparing the trade and autarky situations. In this case, however, it cannot be said that the gain from trade will necessarily be positive. As the reader may confirm, the argument of the previous section can readily be adapted to show that, in this case, the choice of specialisation may or may not be optimal for consumption and that, while a specialisation which is optimal will necessarily yield a positive gain from trade, a non-optimal specialisation may yield a positive, or a zero, or even a negative gain from trade.

Suppose now that $0 < s < 1$. With the wage given as $\bar{w}$ and with $g = sr$, it will be clear that the chosen specialisation, being such as to maximise r, will necessarily be optimal for the rate of growth. Indeed, Fig. 4.5, in which the set of non-negative international prices is divided into regions showing which specialisation will be adopted with $w = \bar{w}$, also shows, for each (P_1, P_2), which specialisation is best in terms of the growth rate, given that $w = \bar{w}$. Similarly, in order to divide that same set of prices into regions showing which specialisation is optimal in terms of consumption per unit of employment, one may find the international prices at which, with $w = \bar{w}$ and $g = sr$, any two given specialisations will yield the same level of consumption, per unit of employment. It is found that, for each of the three pairs of specialisations, these international prices lie on a straight line; the three straight lines, whose positions depend on neither the savings ratio, s, nor the level of the wage rate, $\bar{w}$, intersect at a common point (which is in fact the point at which autarky prices would lie at a zero rate of profit).

We may now suppose that the set of non-negative international prices has been divided into regions, both in terms of which specialisation is optimal for the growth rate (and the profit rate) and in terms of which specialisation is optimal for consumption. At any international prices for which the same specialisation is best for both growth and consumption, one may say unambiguously that capitalists will choose the specialisation which is optimal for both growth and consumption and that the gain from trade is positive. At any other prices, capitalists will choose a technique which is optimal in terms of the growth rate but non-optimal in terms of consumption.

When the choice of specialisation made by capitalists is non-optimal in terms of consumption, there may, in a certain sense, be a loss from trade. Consider the case $m_1 > m_2$, with international prices such that a C specialisation is chosen. In Fig. 5.4, the with-trade consumption level, growth rate and profit rate are shown as c, g and r respectively, the corresponding autarky quantities being $\bar{c}, \bar{g}$ and $\bar{r}$; the solid straight line is the wage–profit (consumption–growth) frontier for a C specialisation. It will be

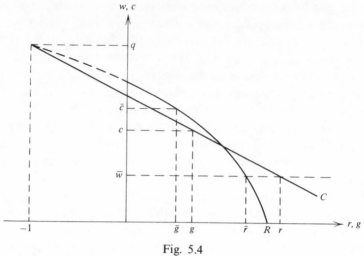

Fig. 5.4

seen that $g > \bar{g}$ but $c < \bar{c}$; the trade situation is superior to autarky in terms of growth but inferior in terms of consumption, per unit of employment. On a straightforward basis, then, one cannot say that there is either a gain or a loss from trade; the position is ambiguous. On the other hand, it may be pointed out that the with-trade consumption–growth combination (c, g) does lie underneath the autarky consumption–growth frontier and that, in this sense, there is a loss from trade. There would be little merit in debating whether the ambiguous or the definitive judgement were the more appropriate.

SUMMARY

With balanced trade, the consumption–growth frontier under any free trade specialisation is precisely dual to the corresponding wage–profit frontier; the analogous result was, of course, established for the closed economy in chapter 3. For any given specialisation, the consumption–growth frontier is higher the greater is productive efficiency in the export industry, the higher is the price (in terms of the consumption commodity) of any machine which is exported and the lower is the price (in the same terms) of any machine which is imported.

With given growth and profit rates, $\bar{g} = s\bar{r}$, the free trade specialisation chosen by capitalists may or may not be optimal in terms of consumption per unit of employment; non-optimality is 'more likely' the smaller is the capitalists' savings ratio, s (being impossible, of course, if $s = 1$). While a consumption-optimal specialisation necessarily yields a positive 'gain from trade', a non-optimal specialisation can yield a positive, a zero or a negative 'gain from trade'; a 'loss from trade' is 'more likely' the smaller is the capitalists' savings ratio, s.

With a given real wage rate, $\bar{w}$, the free trade specialisation will necessarily yield a free trade growth rate greater than the autarky growth rate. In general, however, the level of consumption per unit of employment will also differ as between the free trade and autarky situations, so that a clear-cut overall assessment of the 'gain from trade' is not easily arrived at.

In assessing the above results, the reader will naturally bear in mind their purely comparative dynamic nature; nothing has been said about a path of transition from autarky to free trade (or *vice versa*). It will also be remembered that no account has been taken of any power that the government might have to affect the pattern of output and trade, whether through overtly trade-affecting policies (e.g. tariffs, quotas, multiple exchange rates) or through measures which affect trade less directly—but perhaps just as significantly—by altering, e.g., the growth rate, $\bar{g}$, or the capitalists' effective (post-tax) savings ratio, s.

A READER'S GUIDE

The next two chapters, 6 and 7, deal with the traditional issues of trade policy in a small open economy. These issues are important ones but the analysis is somewhat involved and many readers may prefer, at least on a first reading, to proceed straight to chapter 8, in which it is shown that the presence of a choice of technique, of many commodities, or of non-tradeable commodities does not greatly alter the analysis of trade which was presented in chapter 4. (Chapter 8 is quite independent of chapters 6 and 7.) Indeed, the reader who is anxious to reach the analysis of multi-country international equilibrium as quickly as possible can even omit chapter 8 on a first reading, since chapter 9 and the first half of chapter 10, which both deal with the simple analysis of international equilibrium, are quite independent of chapters 6, 7 and 8. Thus different readers may take different 'routes' through the remaining chapters—though it is to be hoped that they will all, eventually, read every chapter.

6

TARIFF POLICY IN A
SMALL ECONOMY

In the previous two chapters it was assumed that capitalists were free to export or import whatever quantities of commodities they chose and to do so at prices equal to the given international prices, i.e. a situation of free trade was assumed. Foreign trade, however, has long been an object of government policy and is today affected by both government and international policies. As a consequence, international trade theorists have devoted much of their work to analysing the effects on trade of various government activities, a common approach to this analysis being that the effects of tariffs are studied at some length and that subsidies, multiple exchange rates, domestic taxes and import quotas are then shown to have effects very similar to those produced by tariffs. In accord with this practice, the present chapter is devoted to an analysis of import tariffs and the following chapter to an examination of certain other government policies which influence international trade.

It will be assumed that the small country considered faces given international prices, which are not only given independently of that country's volume of trade but are also independent of any tariffs levied in that country. The tariffs levied by the government of the country under consideration will be taken not to discriminate according to the country of origin of imports but will be allowed to discriminate by commodity, so that one has to refer to the 'tariff structure' rather than to 'the tariff rate'. The analysis of the effects of a positive tariff structure will concentrate on the implications for the level of the wage rate and the rate of profit, for the protection of industries and for the revenue generated. All these effects, it will be as well to note from the outset, stem from the fact that tariffs cause domestic price ratios to differ from international price ratios.

As before, the method of analysis will be that of comparative dynamics, the comparison now being between an economy with a higher tariff structure and one with lower—possibly zero—tariffs. Only the differences between these two economies will be considered, any effects of the difference in tariffs on other economies being ignored. It is particularly important to remember that such a comparison does not provide an adequate account of the dynamic effects of *changing* the tariff structure in a given economy; this point will be returned to below.

TARIFFS

Suppose that *ad valorem* tariffs, at rates t_c, t_1 and t_2, are levied on any imports of C, M_1 and M_2 respectively and that any revenue produced is fully used by the government in purchasing the consumption commodity C; it need not be considered here to what purpose the government puts the quantity of C obtained. It will be helpful to set down the relations between prices, wage rate and profit rate that must obtain in a given industry, when it exists, under autarky, under free trade and under with-tariff specialisation. Under autarky, of course, all three industries exist simultaneously; while the free trade and with-tariffs relations are to be interpreted as *alternative* relations, so that those referring to the C industry apply only under a C specialisation, and so on.

For the C industry we have:

Autarky	$w + p_1(1 + r) = q$	(1)
Free trade	$w + P_1(1 + r) = q$	(2)
With tariffs	$w + (1 + t_1)P_1(1 + r) = q$	(3)

For the M_1 industry we have:

Autarky	$w + p_2(1 + r) = m_1 p_1$	(4)
Free trade	$w + P_2(1 + r) = m_1 P_1$	(5)
With tariffs	$(1 + t_c)w + (1 + t_2)P_2(1 + r) = m_1 P_1$	(6)

Finally, for the M_2 industry we have:

Autarky	$w + p_2(1 + r) = m_2 p_2$	(7)
Free trade	$w + P_2(1 + r) = m_2 P_2$	(8)
With tariffs	$(1 + t_c)w + P_2(1 + r) = m_2 P_2$	(9)

Thus relation (3) shows the effect of a tariff on M_1 imports under a C specialisation; (6) that of tariffs on C and M_2 imports under an M_1 specialisation; and (9) that of a tariff on C imports under an M_2 specialisation.

It should be noted that each 'with-tariffs' equation is the same as the corresponding 'free trade' equation, except that any element on the left-hand side which refers to an imported commodity is multiplied by 'one plus the tariff rate'. Now since in each 'with-tariffs' equation, at least one term on the left-hand side is so multiplied, it follows immediately that, for each specialisation, the wage–profit frontier is lower with tariffs than under free trade. It was seen in chapter 4, however, that, under free trade, international prices not equal to autarky prices induce specialisation precisely because such specialisation yields a wage–profit frontier lying unambiguously above the autarky wage–profit pair $(\bar{w}, \bar{r})$. There thus arises the possibility that a 'with-tariffs' wage–profit frontier might lie so far below the 'free trade' frontier as to pass *below* the autarky wage–profit pair $(\bar{w}, \bar{r})$, thus rendering that specialisation unprofitable.

Before considering further the possibility that tariffs might be so high as to render trade unprofitable, it will be convenient to follow the procedure, adopted in chapter 4, of finding which pairs of international prices (P_1, P_2) will leave capitalists indifferent as between two alternative specialisations. It must be noted with care that, by contrast with the situation in chapter 4, such a price pair will *not* imply the possibility of a semi-specialisation, in which two industries exist simultaneously. For, by construction, relations (3), (6) and (9) are alternative relations, in each of which a tariff is levied only on the imports involved in a given specialisation; it would thus be inconsistent to apply, say, (3) and (9) to a situation of semi-specialisation in C and M_2. To emphasise this point, the loci of pairs of prices (P_1, P_2) which leave capitalists indifferent between alternative specialisations will here be called 'lines of alternative specialisation', which are to be distinguished from our earlier 'lines of semi-specialisation'. (Semi-specialisation induced by tariff protection will be discussed later in this chapter.)

At this point it is, of course, necessary to decide whether the wage rate or the profit rate is to be taken as given; the analysis will first be conducted in terms of a given rate of profit, $\bar{r}$, and then be modified to the case of a given wage rate, $\bar{w}$. Setting $r = \bar{r}$ in (3), (6) and (9), it is easy to deduce that the with-tariffs lines of alternative specialisation will be as follows:

$M_1 M_2$ alternative specialisation

$$P_2 = \left[\frac{m_1}{m_2 + (1 + \bar{r})t_2} \right] P_1 \qquad (10)$$

CM_2 alternative specialisation

$$P_2 = (1 + t_c)\left[\frac{q - (1 + \bar{r})(1 + t_1)P_1}{m_2 - (1 + \bar{r})}\right] \qquad (11)$$

CM_1 alternative specialisation

$$P_2 = \left\{\frac{-(1 + t_c)q + [m_1 + (1 + \bar{r})(1 + t_c)(1 + t_1)]P_1}{(1 + \bar{r})(1 + t_2)}\right\} \qquad (12)$$

It will be seen that (10), (11) and (12) are the equations of three straight lines, which naturally reduce to the corresponding equations in chapter 4 when $t_c = t_1 = t_2 = 0$; it may be noted that, by contrast with the situation under free trade, the $M_1 M_2$ line of alternative specialisation does now depend on the value of $\bar{r}$, unless $t_2 = 0$. It can be shown that the three lines of alternative specialisation meet at a common point, as before, but that this point need no longer be the point (p_1, p_2); it is also important to note that the CM_2 line of alternative specialisation passes through the point $P_1 = p_1/(1 + t_1)$, $P_2 = (1 + t_c)p_2$. Thus Fig. 6.1(a) may be drawn. The three lines of alternative specialisation drawn in Fig. 6.1(a) show, it must be remembered, the combinations of P_1 and P_2 at which each of two with-tariff specialisations will yield the same real wage, given $\bar{r}$; they do not show, in the presence of tariffs, whether that wage will exceed the autarky wage, $\bar{w}$.

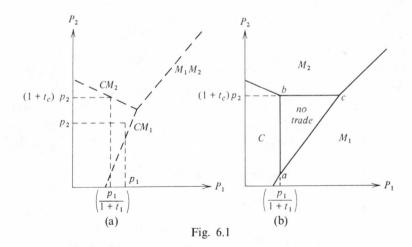

Fig. 6.1

Consider, now, equations (1) and (3); it will be clear that a C specialisation will yield a real wage greater than the autarky wage rate, $\bar{w}$, if and only if $(1 + t_1)P_1 < p_1$. In the same way, using equations (7) and (9), it may be seen that an M_2 specialisation will yield a wage rate greater than $\bar{w}$ if and only if $P_2 > (1 + t_c)p_2$. Hence no pair of international prices (P_1, P_2) lying to the right of ab and below bc in Fig. 6.1(b) will induce either a C specialisation or an M_2 specialisation. It can also be shown that no (P_1, P_2) lying above ac in Fig. 6.1(b) will induce an M_1 specialisation. (The points a, b and c of Fig. 6.1(b) lie on the lines CM_1, CM_2 and M_1M_2, respectively, of Fig. 6.1(a).) Thus, in Fig. 6.1(b), the set of non-negative international prices is now divided up into *four* regions. If international prices should fall in one of the regions marked C, M_1 or M_2 then they will induce capitalists to engage in the corresponding specialisation, just as in the free trade case, the only difference being that, with positive tariffs, the real wage will be smaller than it would be under free trade, while tariff revenue is correspondingly positive. If, however, international prices should fall within the triangle abc, they will not lead capitalists to engage in any specialisation; the economy will remain autarkic with wage rate $\bar{w}$ and with tariff revenue necessarily being zero. (In such a case the tariffs are said to constitute a prohibitive tariff structure, prohibitive, that is, of any international trade.)

If all the tariff rates were zero, the 'no-trade triangle', abc in Fig. 6.1(b), would naturally shrink to the point $P_1 = p_1, P_2 = p_2$. Conversely, it is easy to show that, other things being equal, a higher value for any one of the tariff rates will imply a larger no-trade triangle. (Put more loosely, the higher are tariffs, the more must international prices differ from autarky prices if they are to induce capitalists to engage in international trade.) As higher and higher tariff structures are considered, the no-trade triangle surrounding the autarky price pair (p_1, p_2) expands. (The corresponding diagram will always appear as in Fig. 6.1(b), except that point a will lie in the positive quadrant if and only if $(1 + t_c)(1 + t_1) < m_2/[m_2 - (1 + \bar{r})]$; if t_c and t_1 should be high enough to violate this condition, the diagram will appear as in Fig. 6.2, there being no international prices at which C and M_1 specialisations will yield the same wage rate.) It may also be shown that, other things being equal, a higher value of t_c will imply a larger C area and smaller M_1 and M_2 areas, a higher value of t_1 will imply a smaller C area and larger M_1 and M_2 areas, while a higher t_2 value will imply larger C and M_2 areas but a smaller M_1 area; a higher tariff on any commodity, that is, will reduce the set of international prices leading to a specialisation for

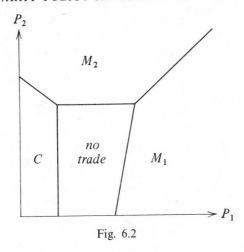

Fig. 6.2

which that commodity is an import, while increasing the set of prices leading to specialisations for which that commodity is not an import.

TARIFFS AND THE PATTERN OF SPECIALISATION

The existence of tariffs does not, of course, only affect whether trade will occur at all; since each with-tariffs line of alternative specialisation is different from the corresponding free trade line of semi-specialisation, even non-prohibitive tariffs may affect the pattern of production. Thus the free trade and the with-tariffs lines of semi-specialisation and of alternative specialisation might appear as the broken and the solid lines, respectively, in Fig. 6.3; the broken lines naturally intersect at $P_1 = p_1, P_2 = p_2$. Comparing two economies with the same technical conditions and rate of profit, $\bar{r}$, one open to free trade and the other open to trade subject to tariffs, it will be seen that if international prices should fall in one of the regions C, M_1 or M_2, then both economies will be trading economies, with the same pattern of specialisation. If international prices should fall in the no-trade triangle abc, other than at the point of autarky prices, the free trade economy will be specialised, or semi-specialised, in the appropriate way, while the with-tariffs economy will be autarkic. If, finally, international prices should lie in one of the three shaded regions in Fig. 6.3, then both economies will be engaged in trade but they will exhibit different patterns of specialisation: for example, if international prices should lie in the 'north-western' shaded area, the free-trading

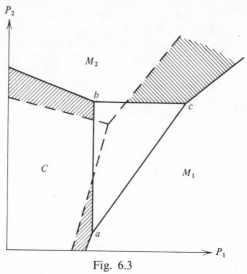

Fig. 6.3

capitalists will adopt an M_2 specialisation, while the capitalists subject to tariffs will adopt a C specialisation. Thus non-prohibitive tariffs may or may not alter the pattern of specialisation adopted at given international prices. The with-tariffs wage rate, given $\bar{r}$, will however always be lower than the free trade wage rate.

TARIFFS WITH A GIVEN WAGE RATE

It remains to be shown how the above analysis must be modified if the wage rate, rather than the rate of profit, is exogenously determined. It may be noted first that, at any (P_1, P_2) lying on an edge of the no-trade triangle discussed above, the appropriate specialisation will, with $r = \bar{r}$, yield the autarky wage rate, $w = \bar{w}$. Now this proposition is clearly reversible and thus the no-trade triangle is the same whether it is the wage rate or the rate of profit that is exogenously given. The lines of alternative specialisation may be obtained by setting $w = \bar{w}$ in (3), (6) and (9) and then, for each pair, finding those prices P_1 and P_2 which yield equal rates of profit. It will be found that, just as with the free trade lines of semi-specialisation, the CM_2 and CM_1 lines of alternative specialisation are sections of conic curves, while the $M_1 M_2$ line of alternative specialisation is a straight line. Each of these lines passes through a corner of the no-trade triangle and the lines meet at a point inside the triangle. Thus,

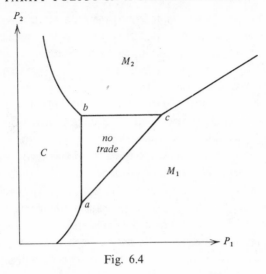

Fig. 6.4

provided that point a lies in the positive quadrant, as discussed above, the set of non-negative international prices may be divided into four regions as shown in Fig. 6.4. (It may be noted that the M_1M_2 line of alternative specialisation in Fig. 6.4 is different from that in Fig. 6.1(b), by contrast with the free-trade situation in which the M_1M_2 line of semi-specialisation is the same whether it is the wage rate or the rate of profit that is given.) The analysis given above for the case of a given rate of profit may now be repeated, *mutatis mutandis*, for the case of a given wage rate. Tariffs may or may not be prohibitive and, when non-prohibitive, may or may not lead to a specialisation different from the free trade specialisation; in every case, however, the with-tariffs rate of profit, given $\bar{w}$, will be lower than the free trade rate of profit.

TARIFFS AND PROTECTION

A major reason for the levying of tariffs is, of course, that the government wishes, for some reason, to maintain the existence of an industry which would not exist under conditions of free trade. Now, as the tariff rates t_c, t_1 and t_2 are (notionally) raised towards infinity, the no-trade triangle expands without limit to absorb the whole set of non-negative international prices. It follows that there exists a tariff structure sufficiently high to bring any pair of (finite) international prices within the no-trade triangle. Thus the government can always maintain the existence of all three industries, i.e. a state of autarky, provided that the consequent restriction of wage and profit rates to the autarky level is politically sustainable.

Of greater practical and theoretical interest, however, is the fact that, by the use of tariffs, the government may be able to lead capitalists to adopt a pattern of semi-specialisation, even at international prices which would lead to complete specialisation under free trade; this less drastic form of protection requires rather more detailed consideration. It must be noted, first, that the phrase 'semi-specialisation' is here used to refer only to semi-specialisation in *production* and not, as previously, to a situation in which capitalists could produce *and export* either or both of two commodities; a tariff structure which is designed to protect an industry, allowing it to exist alongside the free trade exporting industry, may or may not create a situation in which both industries are potential exporters (see below). The method of analysis of tariff protection is perhaps best shown by means of examples, which will show how different industries can be protected at the different sets of international prices marked 1 to 6 in Fig. 6.5, each of which would induce a complete specialisation under free trade conditions. The analysis will be carried out for the case of a given rate of profit, $r = \bar{r}$; the reader may repeat it for the case of a given wage rate.

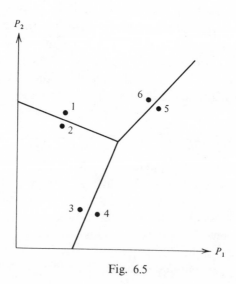

Fig. 6.5

Point 1.   Suppose first, then, that international prices lie at point 1 in Fig. 6.5, so that an M_2 specialisation would be adopted under free trade. If w^F is the free trade wage and w^C the wage rate that would obtain in the hypothetical case of a C specialisation's being adopted then:

$$w^F + P_2(1 + \bar{r}) = m_2 P_2 \tag{13}$$

$$w^F + P_1(1 + \bar{r}) > q \tag{14}$$

$$w^C + P_1(1 + \bar{r}) = q \tag{15}$$

Relations (13) and (15) follow directly from the meaning of w^F and w^C; (14) expresses the fact that the C industry is not viable under free trade.

Consider now the situation in an otherwise similar economy, in which the government protects the existence of a domestic C industry by levying a tariff, at rate t_c, on imports of C; the higher domestic relative price of the C commodity, by comparison with the free trade economy, will enable the C industry to exist as a domestic industry, though it will not be able to export. If the wage rate is w, then;

$$(1 + t_c)w + P_2(1 + \bar{r}) = m_2 P_2 \tag{16}$$

$$(1 + t_c)w + P_1(1 + \bar{r}) = (1 + t_c)q \tag{17}$$

It will be seen immediately from (13) and (16) that

$$(1 + t_c)w = w^F$$

and from (15) and (17) it follows that

$$(1 + t_c)w = (1 + t_c)w^C + t_c P_1(1 + \bar{r})$$

Hence:
$$w^C < w < w^F \tag{18}$$

As is shown in (18), the wage rate in the economy with the protected domestic C industry will lie above the (hypothetical) wage rate w^C but will be lower than the wage rate in the free trade economy. Thus the 'cost' of protecting the domestic C industry is that, with the same profit rate $\bar{r}$, the wage rate is lower than it would be with free trade. (Correspondingly, of course, government revenue is generated by the tariff.)

Point 2.   Suppose now that international prices lie at point 2 in Fig. 6.5, so that a C specialisation will be adopted in a free trade economy. By contrast with the case discussed immediately above, a domestic M_2 industry cannot be protected by the levying of a tariff on imports of its product, since the C specialisation involves no such imports. The M_2

industry can be 'protected' only by leving a tariff on the imports of M_1 required by the C industry, such that the lower wage now generated in the C industry is equal to the free trade wage that would be given by a (hypothetical) M_2 specialisation. With such a tariff, capitalists will be indifferent as between a C and an M_2 specialisation and *both industries* will be potential export industries. This case, then, is qualitatively different from that discussed above.

Extending the notation used above, in an obvious way, the relevant relations for the present case are:

free trade
$$w^F + P_1(1 + \bar{r}) = q$$
$$w^F + P_2(1 + \bar{r}) > m_2 P_2$$
$$w^2 + P_2(1 + \bar{r}) = m_2 P_2$$

with tariffs
$$w + (1 + t_1)P_1(1 + \bar{r}) = q$$
$$w + P_2(1 + \bar{r}) = m_2 P_2$$

It will be clear that $w^2 = w < w^F$. The with-protection wage is lower than the free trade wage, as above, but is now equal to, not greater than, the (hypothetical) alternative specialisation wage since, in this case, the tariff merely penalises the industry which would exist under free trade, without raising the domestic relative price for the 'protected' industry.

Point 3. If international prices should fall at point 3 in Fig. 6.5, so that a C specialisation would be adopted under free trade, a domestic M_1 industry can be protected by the imposition of a tariff, at rate t_1, on imports of M_1. The analysis proceeds much as for the case of prices at point 1 in Fig. 6.5, the relevant relations being, in an obvious notation:

free trade
$$w^F + P_1(1 + \bar{r}) = q$$
$$w^F + P_2(1 + \bar{r}) > m_1 P_1$$
$$w^1 + P_2(1 + \bar{r}) = m_1 P_1$$

with tariffs
$$w + (1 + t_1)P_1(1 + \bar{r}) = q$$
$$w + P_2(1 + \bar{r}) = (1 + t_1)m_1 P_1$$

As the reader may check, it follows immediately that $w^1 < w < w^F$, a result fully analogous to that obtained above for the case of prices at point 1 in in Fig. 6.5.

Point 4. If international prices lie at point 4 in Fig. 6.5, so that an M_1

specialisation would be induced under free trade, a new element is introduced into the analysis in that two tariffs may now be used to protect the domestic C industry. A tariff on C imports will protect the C industry by raising the domestic relative price of its product, while a tariff on M_2 imports will 'protect' the C industry by simply penalising the M_1 industry; thus in this case both the kinds of protection found above may operate at once.

The relevant relations are;

free trade
$$w^F + P_2(1 + \bar{r}) = m_1 P_1$$
$$w^F + P_1(1 + \bar{r}) > q$$
$$w^C + P_1(1 + \bar{r}) = q$$
with tariffs
$$(1 + t_c)w + (1 + t_2)P_2(1 + \bar{r}) = m_1 P_1$$
$$(1 + t_c)w + P_1(1 + \bar{r}) = (1 + t_c)q$$

It follows that $w^C \leq w < w^F$, where $w^C \leq w$ according as $t_c \geq 0$, i.e. the with-tariffs wage is greater than or equal to the (hypothetical) wage w^C according as protection does or does not involve a tariff on the product of the C industry, in addition to any merely penalising tariff on M_2 imports. Only if $t_c = 0$ will C become a potential export industry.

Points 5 and 6. If international prices should fall at point 5 in Fig. 6.5, so that the free trade specialisation would be in M_1, then it is easy to show how a domestic M_2 industry could be protected by the levying of a tariff, at rate t_2, on imports of M_2. The reader may carry out this analysis and show that $w^2 < w < w^F$, which is, of course, the result to be expected in a case, such as the present one, in which protection does not take the form of merely penalising the export industry. If prices should lie at point 6 in Fig. 6.5, however, a third kind of case arises; there is no way of using tariffs to protect a domestic M_1 industry, in such a situation. A tariff on imports of C would certainly imply a real wage rate lower than the free trade rate but would in no way affect the *relative* profitability of the M_1 and M_2 industries, while tariffs on either M_1 or M_2 imports could obviously play no role.

Thus an industry may be protected by the levying of a tariff on imports of its product, in which case the industry can survive as a domestic industry, due to the domestic relative price of its product being above the corresponding international relative price, but cannot be an export industry. Or an industry may be 'protected' by a merely penal tariff on imports required by the free trade export industry, in which case the 'protected' industry can be an export industry. (As was seen above, these two types of protection can coexist, in which case the protected industry cannot be an export industry.) Finally, tariff protection of an industry may be impossible. Whenever it is possible, the 'cost' of such protection is that the real wage rate, with a given profit rate, is lower than the wage rate that would obtain under free trade.

(The reader may now repeat the whole of the above analysis under the assumption that the wage rate is given, as $w = \bar{w}$, to show that, *mutatis mutandis*, all the above results carry over. In particular, whenever tariff protection of a domestic industry is possible, it involves the acceptance of a profit rate which, with the given wage rate, is lower than the profit rate which would obtain under free trade.)

A REMINDER

Since tariffs imply a wage–profit frontier lying below the free trade frontier, it might at first seem puzzling that capitalists and workers sometimes call for tariff protection. Any such puzzlement shows how important it is to remember the comparative dynamics nature of our analysis. It has been shown that if two small economies, with identical production methods and rate of profit (or wage rate), face the same international prices, one of the economies having tariffs and the other not, then the wage rate (or profit rate) will be higher in the free trade economy than in the other. It has *not* been shown how wage and profit rates, and output and employment in particular industries, will move through time in a given economy, as international prices and domestic tariffs change through time. Yet it is just such truly dynamic questions that are usually at stake, when capitalists or workers call for the erection or the maintenance of tariff barriers. For example, if Australian workers argue that they would be harmed by the removal of Australian tariffs on labour-intensive imports, it cannot be claimed that the arguments given above show them to be wrong. At most, the argument that free trade gives the highest wage–profit frontier might be used to show that if a smooth transition from protection to free trade were possible, without long-run loss of jobs and with adequate income maintenance for those temporarily unemployed, then the removal of tariffs would be in the Australian workers' interest. It will be clear that the certainty of such a smooth transition might well be doubted. Thus, while international trade theorists may quite properly draw attention to the wage/profit maximising properties of free trade, they are obliged to recognise that calls for tariff protection are not necessarily based on ignorance of those maximising properties but may stem from legitimate concern with problems of dynamic adjustment.

TARIFFS AND THE GAIN FROM TRADE

It was shown in the previous chapter that the free trade specialisation, induced by given international prices, could be either optimal or non-optimal in terms of consumption and growth and that, when non-optimal, it could be either superior or inferior to autarky. It has now been seen that tariffs may imply the adoption of a policy of autarky and, when not prohibitive, may induce a specialisation different from that adopted under free trade or may be employed for the express purpose of maintaining a semi-specialisation. It follows at once that the gain from trade in an economy with tariffs may be greater or smaller than that in an otherwise similar free trade economy and that the with-tariffs gain may be either positive or negative. Prohibitive tariffs, for example, clearly imply a zero gain from trade but such a 'gain' may be either greater or smaller than the gain that would occur under free trade, according as the latter gain were negative or positive.

If non-prohibitive tariffs are used to maintain a semi-specialisation, at international prices which would, under free trade, induce a complete specialisation then, again, the resulting level of consumption per unit of employment, for a given growth rate $\bar{g}$, may exceed or fall short of the free trade level. It is easy to show that the consumption level with a semi-specialisation will be equal to the weighted average of the consumption levels with the two separate specialisations involved, where the weights are the proportions of total employment given in the two industries. Provided that both weights are positive—that both industries exist—it follows that if the free trade specialisation is optimal for consumption, then the tariff induced semi-specialisation will yield a lower consumption level than free trade, while if the free trade specialisation is non-optimal, the reverse may be the case. Thus while protection will necessarily yield, for given $\bar{r}$, a wage rate lower than that yielded by free trade, it may yield, for given $\bar{g}$, a higher or lower level of consumption per unit of employment.

(The reader may adapt the above remarks to the case of a given wage rate, $\bar{w}$.)

TARIFF REVENUE

While the revenue generated by tariffs is not generally a major consideration in advanced capitalist countries, it is sometimes an important item of government revenue in less-developed capitalist economies. It will only be possible here to consider the tariff revenue arising with a given specialisation, for to analyse the variation of tariff revenue with tariff rates when differences in the latter implied differences in specialisation, would be rather complex. Tariff revenue will be assumed to be entirely spent on government purchases of the consumption commodity and all quantities referred to will be per unit of employment. It is important to remember throughout that, with a given specialisation, the consumption–growth frontier is independent of the tariff rates and that the level of consumption is always the sum of the wage, the tariff revenue and capitalists' consumption: it is the *distribution* of the C commodity which varies with the tariff rates.

Consider two small economies, with identical production methods and rates of profit and growth—given by $\bar{g} = s\bar{r}$—which face the same international prices and, despite differences in their tariff structures, have the same specialisation. Whichever specialisation is in question, the level of consumption will be the same in both economies but the wage rate will be lower in the economy with higher tariffs. (In the case of an M_1 specialisation it will be assumed, for simplicity, that one of the economies has the higher value of both t_c and t_2.) It follows immediately that 'tariff revenue plus capitalists' consumption' will be higher in the higher tariff economy. Tariff revenue will, of course, be higher in the economy with the higher tariffs, being given by $[t_1 P_1(1 + \bar{g})]$ or $[t_2 P_2(1 + \bar{g}) + t_c c]$ or $[t_c c]$ for the C, M_1 and M_2 specialisations respectively. Capitalists' consumption, being proportional to the value of the machines used in production, will be unaffected by a tariff t_c but will be higher the higher is t_1 or t_2; it follows that, the level of consumption being given, the 'wage plus tariff revenue' will be unaffected by the level of t_c but will be lower in the economy with the higher t_1 or t_2. (Hence even if the 'higher-tariff' government redistributed its extra tariff revenue to the workers, it could at best restore their total incomes to the level of wages in the lower tariff economy, and could not even do that if t_1 or t_2 were different as between the two economies.)

Suppose now that the two economies have the same given wage rate, $\bar{w}$, and the same capitalists' savings ratio, s. Both the profit rate and the growth rate will be lower in the higher tariff economy, which will therefore have the higher level of consumption and hence the higher level of 'tariff revenue plus capitalists' consumption'. Now it is easy to show that capitalists' consumption will, in this case, always be lower in the higher tariff economy. It follows immediately that, just as in the case of given growth and profit rates, tariff revenue will always be higher in the economy with higher tariffs.

SUMMARY

This chapter has been concerned with the effects of a tariff *structure*—not just a uniform tariff rate—with tariffs on means of production as well as on the consumption commodity; in the recently fashionable terminology, 'effective'—and not just nominal—tariffs have been considered.

It has been seen that, for any given specialisation, a tariff will lower the wage–profit frontier and thus lower the with-trade profit rate (for a given real wage) or lower the with-trade real wage (for a given rate of profit); there is always a tariff sufficiently high to induce capitalists to choose autarky rather than trade (a 'prohibitive' tariff). *Ceteris paribus*, the higher is the (non-prohibitive) tariff on a commodity, the smaller is the set of international relative prices which will induce a specialisation for which that commodity is an import and the larger is the set of such prices inducing a specialisation in which it is not an import. A change in a non-prohibitive tariff structure may or may not imply a change in the pattern of specialisation.

When tariffs are used to 'protect' an industry, so that the economy has two industries with tariffs whilst it would have only one under free trade, different types of case arise, according as the protected industry is or is not a potential export industry. It will *not* be a potential export industry if its product would be an import under free trade but if, by contrast, its product would not be so imported, tariff 'protection' then simply consists of 'penalising' the free trade industry, with the result that *both* the with-tariffs industries are potential export industries. It was also noted that cases arise in which more than one type of tariff structure is available for the protection of a given industry and that yet other cases occur in which *no* tariff structure is available for the protection of a given industry. In all cases of protection, however, the protected situation yields a lower wage rate (given $\bar{r}$) or a lower profit rate (given $\bar{w}$) than does free trade.

Since the presence of a tariff structure may or may not lead to the adoption of a pattern of output and trade different from the free trade specialisation, it follows from the analysis of chapter 5 that a (prohibitive or non-prohibitive) tariff structure may increase, reduce or leave unchanged the 'gain from trade', relative to a state of free trade. For a non-prohibitive tariff structure, the with-tariffs 'gain from trade', relative to autarky, may be positive, zero or negative. Analogous results hold for 'protective' tariff structures.

A number of (rather restricted) results were also obtained concerning the effect of different tariff structures on the distribution of the available flow of consumption between workers, capitalists and the government.

The reader must always remember, when considering the above results, both that they all stem from the fact that tariffs cause domestic price ratios to differ from the corresponding international price ratios and that they are all of a purely comparative dynamic nature.

7
NON-TARIFF TRADE POLICY
IN A SMALL ECONOMY

As was seen in the last chapter, tariffs cause domestic relative prices to differ from international relative prices, this fact being crucial both to the possibility that tariffs might cause the pattern of production to differ from that prevailing in a free trade economy and to the revenue generating property of (non-prohibitive) tariffs. Now since subsidies, taxes, multiple exchange rates and import quotas also each imply a difference between domestic and international price ratios, it is to be expected that their effects will be comparable to those of tariffs. Comparability, however, is not equivalence and it may be noted at once that while, under tariffs, domestic producers and consumers face the same relative prices, that is not so with subsidies and certain taxes, even though it continues to be true with other taxes, with multiple exchange rates and with import quotas. It should also be remembered that, while all policies are likely to have both trade effects and revenue effects, the adoption of a given policy will in some cases be motivated primarily by the one consideration and in other cases by the second. It remains the case, however, that the analysis of each policy turns on a careful consideration of the effects on domestic relative prices and that it can be presented in terms of the consequent effects on the wage–profit frontiers involved.

It would be tedious, rather than instructive, to work through the analysis of many different combinations and applications of trade-affecting policies. No attempt at thoroughness will therefore be made in this chapter; it will suffice to indicate the method of analysis required in each case and to leave to readers the task of applying those methods to the consideration of situations which particularly interest them. Again in the interest of brevity, the analysis given below will, for the most part, be restricted to the case of given rates of profit and growth ($\bar{g} = s\bar{r}$), it being left to the reader to consider what modifications to the argument might be required if, by contrast, it were the wage rate ($\bar{w}$) that were given. The effects of different policies will be illustrated with respect to the various alternative positions

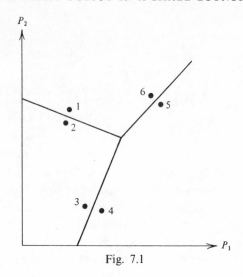

Fig. 7.1

of international prices, relative to the free trade lines of semi-specialisation, shown in Fig. 7.1, which reproduces Fig. 6.5.

SUBSIDIES

Subsidies may be used to cause the pattern of specialisation to differ from that under free trade and they may be used to maintain a pattern of semi-specialisation that would not occur under free trade; just as tariffs may be so used. Subsidies nevertheless differ from tariffs in a number of respects, a major one being that, unlike tariffs, subsidies to producers lead the latter to face domestic relative prices which differ from those faced by consumers. It should also be noted that while a tariff may serve to protect the existence of a domestic industry, it cannot enable that industry to export, if it is a tariff on that industry's product; subsidies, however, if they enable an industry to survive in the face of imports at world prices, necessarily enable it to export at world prices. Again, while tariffs can necessarily be levied only on imports, subsidies can be paid either on domestic production or on imports—though it is true that this asymmetry is removed when a tariff is regarded as merely one tax among many, for domestic production can, of course, be taxed. Finally, while a (non-prohibitive) tariff generates government revenue, the paying of a subsidy constitutes government expenditure and one is inevitably led to ask how the subsidy is financed.

Consider first how subsidies might imply a specialisation, at given world prices, different from the free trade specialisation. It will be convenient to ignore, at present, the question how the subsidy is financed—it might, for example, be financed by the levying of a tax, such as a uniform tax on wages, which has no influence on the pattern of specialisation. Suppose, then, that the government will subsidise domestic production at the *ad valorem* rate s_i ($i = C, 1, 2$) in the C, M_1 and M_2 industries respectively and will subsidise imports of C, M_1 and M_2 at the *ad valorem* rates $s_i'(i = C, 1, 2)$. The alternative wage–profit frontiers at international prices (P_1, P_2), will be as follows:

C specialisation $\qquad\qquad w + (1 - s_1')P_1(1 + \bar{r}) = (1 + s_c)q$ $\qquad$ (1)

M_1 specialisation $\quad (1 - s_c')w + (1 - s_2')P_2(1 + \bar{r}) = (1 + s_1)m_1 P_1$ $\qquad$ (2)

M_2 specialisation $\quad (1 - s_c')w + \qquad\quad P_2(1 + \bar{r}) = (1 + s_2)m_2 P_2$ $\qquad$ (3)

(It should be noted that if we set $s_i = 0$ and $s_i' = - t_i (i = C, 1, 2)$, then (1), (2) and (3) become the with-tariffs equations (3), (6) and (9) of chapter 6; thus subsidies on imports may be thought of as negative tariffs. Subsidies on domestic production have their counterpart not in tariffs but in domestic taxes on production, as will be seen below.)

From (1), (2) and (3) it is not difficult to deduce which specialisation will maximise the wage—and will therefore be adopted—at any given international prices and rates of subsidy. International prices lying on the line,

$$P_2 = \left[\frac{(1 + s_1)m_1}{(1 + s_2)m_2 - (1 + \bar{r})s_2'} \right] P_1$$

for example, will leave capitalists indifferent as between an M_1 and an M_2 specialisation; note how subsidies to M_1 production and to the importation of M_2 push this line above the free trade $M_1 M_2$ line of semi-specialisation, $P_2 = (m_1/m_2)P_1$, while a subsidy to M_2 production has the opposite effect. The reader may easily continue the analysis, so as to divide the set of non-negative international prices by three with-subsidies lines of alternative specialisation, meeting at a common point which will not, in general, be the point $P_1 = p_1$, $P_2 = p_2$. (Subsidies do not, of course, create a 'no-trade triangle'.) It will then be clear which specialisation will be adopted, for given subsidies and international prices, and that that specialisation may differ, at given prices, as between two (otherwise equal) economies with different subsidy structures.

If attention is to be focussed on the relations between the given profit rate, $\bar{r}$, subsidies and the pattern of trade, rather than on the role of international prices, then the analysis is best conducted by means of the alternative technique introduced at the end of chapter 4. With given international prices, the wage–profit frontiers (1), (2) and (3) may be drawn, for zero subsidies, so that the free trade specialisation for each possible $\bar{r}$ may be seen. Subsidies may then be introduced and will, of course, raise each wage–profit frontier; note that production subsidies raise the heights of the three frontiers, while import subsidies alter their slopes. The reader may carry out this analysis, for alternative given international prices, noting how the pattern of specialisation adopted depends on the profit rate, $\bar{r}$, on P_1 and P_2 and on the subsidy structure.

AN EXAMPLE

The analysis of the use of subsidies to maintain an industry that would not exist under free trade conditions, may be illustrated by the following example, which shows both how an industry might be protected by the combined use of tariffs and subsidies and how the tariff revenue and subsidy expenditure can be made equal, so that protection is 'self-financing'.

Suppose then that international prices lie at point 1 in Fig. 7.1; under free trade an M_2 specialisation would be adopted. If the government wishes to maintain the C industry in existence as a domestic, though not an exporting, industry, it could do this by levying a tariff on imports of the C commodity, at rate t_c, and granting a subsidy on imports of the M_1 machine, required by the domestic C industry for production purposes, at rate s_1'.

Let w^F be the wage that would obtain under free trade and w the wage obtaining under protection of the C industry; let w^C be the wage that would exist in the hypothetical case of a C specialisation's being chosen under free trade. Then:

$$w^F + P_2(1 + \bar{r}) = m_2 P_2 \tag{4}$$

$$w^F + P_1(1 + \bar{r}) > q \tag{5}$$

$$w^C + P_1(1 + \bar{r}) = q \tag{6}$$

It will be seen that $w^F > w^C$, which is, of course, simply a way of stating that an M_2 specialisation would be the free trade choice. Now the C industry will be able to survive as a domestic industry if:

$$(1 + t_c)w + P_2(1 + \bar{r}) = m_2 P_2 \tag{7}$$

$$(1 + t_c)w + (1 - s_1')P_1(1 + \bar{r}) = (1 + t_c)q \tag{8}$$

On comparing (7) with (4) and (8) with (6), it will be seen that $w^C < w < w^F$; the C industry is protected at the 'cost' of the wage rate, w, being lower than the free trade wage rate.

Now let L be total employment and L_c, L_2 be employment in the C and M_2 industries respectively. Trade will be balanced if:

$$P_2[m_2 - (1 + \bar{g})]L_2 = P_1(1 + \bar{g})L_c + (cL - qL_c) \tag{9}$$

i.e. if the export earnings of the M_2 industry equal the cost of importing M_1 machines plus the cost of importing the excess of total consumption over domestic C production. Total tariff revenue, T, will be given by:

$$T = t_c(cL - qL_c) \tag{10}$$

while total subsidy payments, S, will be given by

$$S = s_1'P_1(1 + \bar{g})L_c \tag{11}$$

Hence (9) may be written as

$$P_2[m_2 - (1 + \bar{g})]L_2 = S/s_1' + T/t_c$$

and, subject to balanced trade, $T \gtreqless S$ according as

$$P_2[m_2 - (1 + \bar{g})]L_2 \gtreqless \left(\frac{1}{s_1'} + \frac{1}{t_c} \right)S$$

or, from (11),

$$L_2 \gtreqless \left\{ \frac{[1 + (s_1'/t_c)]P_1(1 + \bar{g})}{P_2[m_2 - (1 + \bar{g})]} \right\} L_c \tag{12}$$

As will be seen from (12), for given rates of tariff and subsidy, tariff revenue will exceed, equal or fall short of subsidy expenditure according to the relative sizes of the M_2 and C industries, as measured by employment, with subsidy outlay naturally being greater, in relation to tariff revenue, the greater is the relative size of the subsidised C industry. Conversely, if L_2 and L_c are taken as given, the relative sizes of T and S will depend on the ratio of the rates t_c and s_1'. Thus when satisfied as an equality, (12) shows what combinations of t_c and s_1' will serve to yield a 'self-financing' system of protection for M_2 and C industries of given size. It will be seen that the greater is (L_c/L_2), the greater must be (t_c/s_1').

Returning to (8), it is clear that w is positively related to s_1' but inversely related to t_c. Thus the greater the relative size of the C industry which is to be protected by the 'self-financing' combination of tariff t_c and subsidy s_1', the lower is the corresponding real wage, i.e. the greater is the 'cost' of protection, in terms of the wage rate, by comparison with the free trade situation.

The reader may carry out similar analyses for the cases of international prices falling at points 2 to 6 in Fig. 7.1; with prices at point 3, for example, the M_1 industry could be maintained as a domestic, but not exporting, industry by the combination of a tariff on M_1 imports, a subsidy to M_1 production and a subsidy on the M_2 imports required for production in the M_1 industry. It should be noted that while, as was seen in chapter 6, the M_1 industry cannot be protected by tariffs alone if prices are at point 6 in Fig. 7.1, it can be made competitive with the M_2 industry as an export industry, by means of a production subsidy.

TAXES

A tariff may properly be regarded as a tax on imports and a production subsidy, as will be seen below, may be thought of as a negative tax on production. It is not to be expected, then, that the analysis of taxes will add a great deal to the analysis of tariffs and subsidies carried out above. It will suffice here to indicate quite briefly how taxes on production and consumption and taxes on wages and profits will affect the wage–profit frontiers for each specialisation and may thereby alter the specialisation induced by given international prices. The emphasis given here to the possible effect of taxation on the pattern of trade does not, of course, involve a denial of the fact that many taxes are levied principally for revenue purposes, their impact on trade being merely a side-effect. This impact is still worthy of consideration, even if it was unintended by the government, and by no means all taxes are levied solely for 'non-trade' purposes.

Taxes on production

Suppose that the government levies a tax at rate $T_i(i = C, 1, 2)$ on the production of industry i (when it exists). The wage–profit frontiers for the alternative specialisations will be:

C specialisation $w + P_1(1 + \bar{r}) = (1 - T_c)q$ (13)

M_1 specialisation $w + P_2(1 + \bar{r}) = (1 - T_1)m_1P_1$ (14)

M_2 specialisation $w + P_2(1 + \bar{r}) = (1 - T_2)m_2P_2$ (15)

It may be noted first that (13), (14) and (15) are identical to (1), (2) and (3) if, in the latter set of equations, we set $s_i' = 0$ and $s_i = -T_i(i = C, 1, 2)$. Thus production taxes are equivalent to negative production subsidies and *vice versa*. Just as production subsidies raise the wage–profit frontiers, leaving their slopes unchanged, so production taxes lower the frontiers, again with unaltered slopes.

The equations (13), (14) and (15), for the with-tax economy, are precisely the equations that would hold for a no-tax economy with output coefficients $(1 - T_c)q, (1 - T_1)m_1$ and $(1 - T_2)m_2$ in the C, M_1 and M_2 industries respectively. It follows at once that the lines of semi-specialisation for the with-tax economy are simply those given above for the no-tax economy (the equations (1), (2) and $m_2P_2 = m_1P_1$ in chapter 4) with q, m_1 and m_2 replaced by $(1 - T_c)q, (1 - T_1)m_1$ and $(1 - T_2)m_2$ respectively. These lines will, of course, meet not at the point (p_1, p_2) but at the point $P_1 = p_1^T$, $P_2 = p_2^T$, where p_1^T, p_2^T are the prices in an autarkic economy with profit rate $\bar{r}$ and production taxes T_c, T_1, T_2. (p_1^T and p_2^T will not, in general, be equal to p_1, p_2 and, indeed, even (p_2^T/p_1^T) will differ from (p_2/p_1) unless $T_1 = T_2$.) The effects of a difference in a given tax rate, as between two otherwise identical economies, that difference being equivalent to a difference in the corresponding output coefficients, has already been analysed in Fig. 4.3. Other things being equal, a higher rate of taxation on the production of a given industry, will imply a smaller set of international prices which will induce a specialisation in that industry. The reader may derive the lines of semi-specialisation with production taxes, see how they vary according to the tax rates and thus check that the specialisation adopted, at given international prices, may vary according to the structure of production taxes.

It is not difficult to show how, revenue considerations aside, production taxes could be used to maintain two industries as actual or potential export industries, at international prices which would induce a complete specialisation in an otherwise identical no-tax economy. For example, with production taxes the M_1M_2 line of semi-specialisation is given by

$$P_2 = \left[\frac{(1 - T_1)m_1}{(1 - T_2)m_2}\right]P_1 \tag{16}$$

and it is clear that this line will lie above or below the corresponding line for a no-tax economy according as $T_1 \lessgtr T_2$. Thus if prices lie at point 5 in Fig. 7.1, an M_1 specialisation will be adopted in a no-tax economy but capitalists can be made indifferent as between M_1 and M_2 specialisations by the levying of a production tax on M_1; from (16), the necessary tax rate, with $T_2 = 0$, will be given by

$$T_1 = \left[\frac{m_1P_1 - m_2P_2}{m_1P_1}\right]$$

In the same way, if prices lie at point 6 in Fig. 7.1, the M_1 industry can be maintained by the levying of a production tax on the M_2 industry, at the rate, with $T_1 = 0$, given by

$$T_2 = \left[\frac{m_2P_2 - m_1P_1}{m_2P_2}\right]$$

In each case, of course, the levying of the tax implies, *via* (14) and (15), that the real wage rate will be lower than it would have been under free trade. The 'cost' of maintaining an industry, in terms of the wage rate, will be greater the 'further away' from the no-tax line of semi-specialisation are the given international prices.

A consumption tax

If a tax is levied, at rate T, on purchases of the consumption commodity C, whether that commodity has been imported or produced domestically, the wage–profit frontiers for the alternative specialisations will be:

C specialisation $(1 + T)w + P_1(1 + r) = q$ \hfill (17)

M_1 specialisation $(1 + T)w + P_2(1 + r) = m_1P_1$ \hfill (18)

M_2 specialisation $(1 + T)w + P_2(1 + r) = m_2P_2$ \hfill (19)

Relations (18) and (19) are necessarily identical to the corresponding relations (6) and (9) of chapter 6, when the only tariff involved is one on the importation of commodity C, levied at the rate $t_c = T$; for in either an M_1 or an M_2 specialisation the consumption commodity is necesarily imported and there is then no significant difference between a tariff on C and a consumption tax. Relation (17), however, does not correspond to a with-tariff relation since a tariff cannot be levied on C when that commodity is being exported and not imported.

It will be clear that if the rate of profit is given and equal to $\bar{r}$ in (17), (18) and (19), then the lines of semi-specialisation will be just the same as those for an otherwise identical economy with no consumption tax, since the specialisation which maximises $(1 + T)w$, at given international prices, will also be the specialisation which maximises w. In this case, then, the consumption tax can have no influence on the choice of specialisation and merely effects a transfer from workers to the government.

On the other hand, if the wage rate is given and equal to $\bar{w}$ in (17), (18) and (19), then while the $M_1 M_2$ line of semi-specialisation will be the same as for a no-tax economy, the CM_1 and CM_2 lines will not. This is simply because those lines depend on the level of $\bar{w}$, in a no-tax economy, and the with-tax economy is precisely equivalent, in the relevant respects, to a no-tax economy with a given wage rate of $(1 + T)\bar{w}$. Hence, with a given wage rate, the choice of specialisation, at given international prices, may vary according to the level of the consumption tax. The reader may now show that, depending on whether $m_1 \gtrless m_2$, it may or may not be possible to levy a consumption tax such that the with-tax lines of semi-specialisation pass through points such as 1, 2, 3 and 4 in Fig. 7.1, i.e. that it may or may not be possible to maintain the existence of an industry, which would not exist under free trade, by means of a consumption tax. When such a policy is possible and is activated it will, of course, yield a rate of profit smaller than the rate that would have obtained under free trade.

A tax on wages

Suppose now that, when it exists, industry i has to pay a tax on its wage bill at rate $t_i^w (i = C, 1, 2)$; the wage–profit frontiers will be:

C specialisation	$(1 + t_c^w)w + P_1(1 + r) = q$	(20)
M_1 specialisation	$(1 + t_1^w)w + P_2(1 + r) = m_1 P_1$	(21)
M_2 specialisation	$(1 + t_2^w)w + P_2(1 + r) = m_2 P_2$	(22)

It will be noted at once that if $t_i^w = T$ in each of (20), (21) and (22), then those relations become identical to the corresponding with-consumption-tax relations above; hence there is no need to consider here the case of a uniform tax on wages. Given that the tax is a differential one, it is easy to see from (20), (21) and (22) that, whether the wage rate or the profit rate is taken to be exogenously determined, the lines of semi-specialisation will all differ from the corresponding no-tax lines of semi-specialisation. It follows that the levying of a differential tax on wages may affect the choice of specialisation, at given international prices, and that such a policy may be used to maintain an industry which would not exist under no-tax conditions—always at the 'cost' of a wage rate or profit rate lower than would obtain under free trade.

A tax on profits

Suppose, finally, that a uniform tax is levied on profits, such that post-tax profits in an industry, when it exists, are a fraction $(1 + t^p)^{-1}$ of pre-tax profits. If r is now taken to represent the profit rate *net* of tax, the wage–profit frontiers will be

$$C \quad \text{specialisation} \quad w + P_1[1 + (1 + t^p)r] = q \tag{23}$$

$$M_1 \text{ specialisation} \quad w + P_2[1 + (1 + t^p)r] = m_1 P_1 \tag{24}$$

$$M_2 \text{ specialisation} \quad w + P_2[1 + (1 + t^p)r] = m_2 P_2 \tag{25}$$

If the wage rate is exogenously given as $\bar{w}$, then it will be seen, from (23), (24) and (25), that the lines of semi-specialisation will be just the same as those for a no-tax economy, since the specialisation which maximises $(1 + t^p)r$, at given international prices, will also maximise r. In this case, then, the uniform profits tax has no influence on the choice of specialisation and merely effects a transfer from the capitalists to the government; the analogy with the case of a uniform tax on wages, or a consumption tax, will be clear. (Of course, if the profits tax should discriminate between industries, rather than being uniform as assumed above, then all the lines of semi-specialisation will differ from the corresponding no-tax lines.)

On the other hand, if the net profit rate is exogenously given as $\bar{r}$, then the CM_1 and CM_2 lines of semi-specialisation will differ from the corresponding no-tax lines, although the $M_1 M_2$ line will not. (Even the $M_1 M_2$ line would differ if the rate of profits tax differed as between the M_1 and M_2 industries.) There is no need to analyse here the precise effects of different uniform tax rates on the positions of the lines of semi-specialisation, for such tax differences are clearly equivalent to profit rate differences as between no-tax economies and the effects of such differences have already been shown in Fig. 4.4, to which the reader should refer, giving the required new interpretation to the diagrams. It will be clear that the choice of specialisation, at given international prices, may vary according to the rate of taxation on profits, even when that rate is uniform.

The reader is recommended to work through the analysis of the taxes considered above, using the alternative technique introduced at the end of chapter 4, by drawing the three no-tax wage–profit frontiers for the no-tax case and then appropriately modifying them for each type of tax. Once the principles of both types of analysis have been firmly grasped, on the basis of the examples given above, the reader should have no difficulty in analysing the effects on trade of other types of taxation.

MULTIPLE EXCHANGE RATES

For the most part, it is assumed throughout this work that the rate of exchange between domestic and foreign currencies is independent of how the foreign currency sold to, or purchased from, the Central Bank was earned or is to be used; this explains, in part, why so little mention is made of the exchange rate, its real world significance notwithstanding. It is necessary here, however, to analyse the effects of a policy of maintaining 'multiple' exchange rates, in which the rate of exchange at which the Central Bank is ready to buy or sell foreign currency, in exchange for domestic currency, does depend on how that foreign currency has been earned or is to be used. Since such a policy will clearly cause domestic relative prices to differ from international relative prices, it is to be expected that it will have effects on trade comparable to those of tariffs and subsidies. Comparable revenue or government expenditure effects will also arise, for even if trade is balanced in terms of foreign currency, so that the Central Bank buys and sells equal quantities of foreign exchange, the Bank's accounts may still show unequal receipts and expenditures in terms of domestic currency.

Suppose, for example, that e_i units of domestic currency are exchanged for one unit of a representative foreign currency, when that foreign currency is required for importing, or has been earned by exporting, commodity $i(i = C, 1, 2)$. The wage–profit frontiers for the alternative specialisations will be:

C specialisation $e_c w + e_1 P_1 (1 + \bar{r}) = e_c q$ (26)

M_1 specialisation $e_c w + e_2 P_2 (1 + \bar{r}) = e_1 m_1 P_1$ (27)

M_2 specialisation $e_c w + e_2 P_2 (1 + \bar{r}) = e_2 m_2 P_2$ (28)

If $e_c = e_1 = e_2$, then (26), (27) and (28) naturally reduce to the corresponding free trade relations. Whether the e_i are equal or not, it is easy to show that the implied lines of semi-specialisation are

$$M_1 M_2 \quad P_2 = \left[\frac{e_1 m_1}{e_2 m_2} \right] P_1 \tag{29}$$

$$CM_2 \quad P_2 = \left\{ \frac{e_c q - e_1 (1 + \bar{r}) P_1}{e_2 [m_2 - (1 + \bar{r})]} \right\} \tag{30}$$

$$CM_1 \quad P_2 = \left[\frac{-e_c q + e_1 (m_1 + 1 + \bar{r}) P_1}{e_2 (1 + \bar{r})} \right] \tag{31}$$

It should be noted that, by comparison with the corresponding free trade line, the slope of each line of semi-specialisation has been multiplied by (e_1/e_2), while the constant term, if any, has been multiplied by (e_c/e_2). The three lines meet at the point

$$P_1 = \left[\frac{e_c}{e_1} \right] p_1, \quad P_2 = \left[\frac{e_c}{e_2} \right] p_2 \tag{32}$$

No 'no-trade triangle' is created, so that the set of non-negative international prices is divided up as shown in Fig. 7.2 (If the Central Bank's exchange rate policy discriminated not only between commodities but also according to whether a particular commodity were being imported or exported, then a 'no-trade triangle' could be created; the reader may adapt the present analysis for the consideration of such a policy.)

It will be clear from Fig. 7.2 that the common point of the lines of semi-specialisation, that is the pair of international prices at which all three specialisations will be equally profitable, can be 'placed' anywhere in the diagram, by a suitable choice of relative exchange rates. More precisely, it follows from (32) that the common point will lie at $(\bar{P}_1, \bar{P}_2)$ provided that

$$e_1 = (p_1/\bar{P}_1) e_c \text{ and } e_2 = (p_2/\bar{P}_2) e_c \tag{33}$$

Hence, for any given international prices, there exists a multiple exchange rate structure which will make all three specialisations equally profitable and which can therefore maintain the existence of all three industries. The

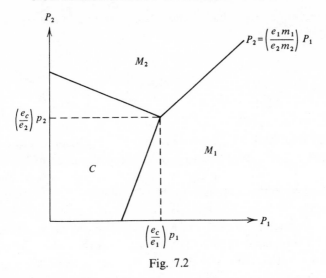

Fig. 7.2

'cost' of such maintenance of industries, however, will be that the wage rate will necessarily be equal to the autarky wage rate, which will, of course, be lower than the free trade wage rate.

By a simple extension of the argument that the point of intersection in Fig. 7.2 may be 'placed' at any point in the diagram, it may be shown that, by a suitable choice of relative exchange rates, any pair of international prices (P_1, P_2) may be brought within any of the three specialisation regions in Fig. 7.2, or made to lie on any of the three lines of semi-specialisation. It follows that a multiple exchange rate policy can be used to maintain two industries, where only one would exist under free trade.

To illustrate this last assertion, suppose that international prices lie at point 3 in Fig. 7.1, so that a C specialisation will be adopted under free trade. If w^F is the free trade wage rate and w^1 the wage rate which would obtain if (hypothetically) an M_1 specialisation were adopted under free trade conditions, then

$$w^F + P_1(1 + \bar{r}) = q \tag{34}$$

$$w^F + P_2(1 + \bar{r}) > m_1 P_1 \tag{35}$$

$$w^1 + P_2(1 + \bar{r}) = m_1 P_1 \tag{36}$$

The Central Bank can support the existence of the M_1 industry by agreeing to buy or sell currency for exporting or importing M_1 at rate e_1, while buying or selling at an exchange rate of unity for other purposes, provided that

$$w + e_1 P_1(1 + \bar{r}) = q \tag{37}$$

$$w + P_2(1 + \bar{r}) = e_1 m_1 P_1 \tag{38}$$

From relations (34) to (38) it is easy to show that $e_1 > 1$ and that $w^F > w > w^1$. The former result is to be expected, since the domestic M_1 industry will be favoured both by the lowering of the domestic price of C relative to its input M_1 and by the raising of the domestic price of M_1 relative to its input M_2, and the second result is, of course, similar to results obtained above in the analysis of tariffs and subsidies. As may be checked by the reader, if trade is balanced, the Central Bank will receive more domestic currency for its sales of foreign exchange than it will have to spend in its purchasing of foreign exchange. Thus the maintenance of the M_1 industry, by the multiple exchange rate policy, may be said to involve a 'tax' in terms of domestic currency, this being another way of saying that the wage rate implied by the policy will fall short of that which would obtain under free trade.

IMPORT QUOTAS

While it is rather obvious that tariffs, subsidies, multiple exchange rates, etc., change domestic relative prices, it might be less immediately clear that import quotas, being controls on physical quantities, will also have that effect. Yet, since the usual purpose of an import quota is the maintenance of an industry which would not exist under free trade conditions, that quota must render equally profitable two industries which would otherwise not be so and it can only do that by changing domestic relative prices. It will be seen below, in fact, that an import quota is, in certain respects, precisely equivalent to a tariff; a major difference between a tariff and a quota being, however, that while the former gives rise to government revenue, the latter may, in effect, grant a 'tariff revenue' to the holder of an import licence.

Import quotas can take various forms and it must suffice here to indicate how the effects of two particular types of import quota may be analysed, i.e. quotas placing a ceiling on the absolute quantity of a commodity which may be imported and quotas restricting the imports of a commodity to a certain proportion of the total domestic absorption of that commodity. Once the principles of the analysis have been grasped, the reader should have no difficulty in extending it to cover other types of import quota. (Export quotas, it should be noted, are usually imposed in an attempt to change international prices and it would therefore be inappropriate to consider them in this chapter.) Suppose, then, that international prices lie at point 1 in Fig. 7.1, so that an M_2 specialisation would be chosen under free trade. With the notation adopted above, the following relations must obtain in a free trade economy:

$$w^F + P_2(1 + \bar{r}) = m_2 P_2 \tag{39}$$

$$w^F + P_1(1 + \bar{r}) > q \tag{40}$$

$$w^C + P_1(1 + \bar{r}) = q \tag{41}$$

In an economy with an effective quota, of whatever form, restricting the the importation of the C commodity, however, the following must hold

$$p_c w + P_2(1 + \bar{r}) = m_2 P_2 \tag{42}$$

$$p_c w + P_1(1 + \bar{r}) = p_c q \tag{43}$$

where p_c is the domestic price of C relative to the international price of C, when the unit of domestic currency is so chosen that the exchange rate is unity. By subtracting (39) from (40) and (42) from (43) and comparing the two results, it is easy to show that

$$p_c > 1$$

The consumption commodity has a higher relative price domestically than internationally, it being precisely this effect of the quota that 'protects' the domestic C industry, which would not exist under free trade. Given that $p_c > 1$, it is easy to see from (39) to (43) that $w^C < w < w^F$; as has been found repeatedly above, the maintenance of an industry involves having a wage rate lower than the wage rate which would obtain under free trade.

If p_c is replaced by $(1 + t_c)$ in (42) and (43), those relations become precisely the with-tariff equations that apply when, with international prices at point 1 in Fig. 7.1, the C industry is protected by a tariff on C imports (see (16), (17) of chapter 6); in this sense, then, one may say that an import quota is equivalent to a tariff. However, whereas the government receives the difference between the domestic and international prices of the imported commodity when a tariff is imposed, under a quota scheme this difference accrues to the capitalists who hold the licences to import — since they purchase the commodity at the (lower) international price but sell it at the (higher) domestic price — if they do not have to pay for the licences. If the importing capitalists do have to pay for their licences, then the 'revenue' will be shared between the licence-holding capitalists and the government, in proportions determined by the price paid for the right to import one unit of the C commodity. If the government charges the maximum price at which all licences will find purchasers, then all the 'revenue' will go to the government, just as it would with an equivalent tariff on C imports.

If the permitted quota of C imports be $\bar{c}$ per unit of employment then, using the notation given above, trade will be balanced if

$$P_2[m_2 - (1 + \bar{g})]L_2 = P_1(1 + \bar{g})L_c + \bar{c}L \qquad (44)$$

while consumption per unit of employment will be given by

$$c = \bar{c} + q(L_c/L) \qquad (45)$$

Relation (44) defines the quota necessary to maint⁻ᵒ ᵘᵃy given relative size of the C and M_2 industries; from (44) and (45) it may be shown that c will lie between the consumption levels that would obtain with C and M_2 specialisations respectively and that it can exceed or fall short of the latter level.

If, on the other hand, the government stipulates that a proportion k of the total consumption of C must be domestically produced ($0 < k < 1$) then the relations corresponding to (44) and (45) will be

$$P_2[m_2 - (1 + \bar{g})]L_2 = P_1(1 + \bar{g})L_c + (1 - k)cL \qquad (46)$$
$$kcL = qL_c \qquad (47)$$

(46) and (47) together define the proportion k necessary for the maintenance of any given relative size of the C and M_2 levels of employment and may, again, be used to show that c will lie between the alternative specialisation levels of consumption per unit of employment.

SUMMARY

Even though only selected examples of non-tariff trade policies have been examined above, the present chapter may have seemed to present an *ad hoc* list of topics, rather than a coherent treatment of a single topic. A summary of the *common* features of the various different topics treated may therefore be of greater use than a detailed topic by topic summary. Subsidies, taxes, multiple exchange rates and quotas were all considered but in each case, domestic relative prices were found to diverge from international relative prices for producers (and in most cases for consumers as well) and it was found that the 'protection' of an industry, by whatever means, always involved a 'cost', in the sense that the implied wage rate was lower than that sustainable under free trade. The effect of 'protection' on consumption per unit of employment, however, was in each case unknown *a priori*, depending on whether the free trade specialisation was or was not efficient in terms of consumption. Again, each type of policy was found to have implications for government revenue and/or government expenditure.

It should be noted that no comment has been made concerning the purely administrative advantages and disadvantages of each type of policy. Nor has consideration been given to the possibility that policies may only be partially effective — tariffs may be avoided by smuggling, false declarations may be made under subsidy and multiple exchange rate schemes, taxes may be evaded, etc. This is not because such matters are unimportant aspects of trade policy — they are not — but because they can only be usefully discussed in a given, specific context. It should also be noted carefully that the above analysis of various trade policies carries with it no implicit advocacy of the adoption or the avoidance of such policies. Policies can only be chosen in the light of given aims and it should not be the business of the international trade theorist to engage in the covert recommendation of aims of economic policy.

8

SOME COMPLICATIONS

It need hardly be said that the foregoing analysis is highly simplified, abstraction having been made from any number of real world complexities. In this chapter a brief indication will be given of how the analysis of a small economy can be modified to allow for the existence of a choice of production methods, of a multiplicity of commodities and of non-traded goods. Attention will be confined to the effects of these phenomena on the pattern of trade and the gain from trade; it will be left to the reader to consider how the analysis of trade policy must be modified.

It may be said at once that neither the general nature of the arguments used nor that of the conclusions reached is greatly modified by the introduction of these complications.

CHOICE OF TECHNIQUE

No attention has been paid so far to how the existence of alternative methods of production may affect the analysis of international trade in a small, open economy. To indicate how this complication may be dealt with, it will suffice to consider the two kinds of technique choice discussed in chapter 3, part II and to restrict attention to the case of an exogenously given growth rate and hence a determined profit rate, $\bar{r}$.

Different M_1 machines

Suppose first that there are two different types of M_1 machine which can be used in the production of the C commodity, each of them being produced by means of the same kind of M_2 machine, which is also used in producing new M_2 machines. Let the two alternative techniques for the (direct and indirect) production of C be defined by $T \equiv (m_2, m_1, q)$ and $T' \equiv (m_2, m'_1, q')$ and suppose that $\bar{r}$ is such that technique T will be in use in an autarkic economy. If p'_1 is the value that an M'_1 machine would have if technique T' were to be adopted in autarkic economy, while P'_1 is the value of an M'_1 machine on the world market, then the following relations must hold, where, as usual, the autarky relations all hold simultaneously, while the free trade relation are alternatives to one another:

Autarky	Free trade	
$\bar{w} + p_2(1 + \bar{r}) = m_2 p_2$	$w + P_2(1 + \bar{r}) = m_2 P_2$	(1)
$\bar{w} + p_2(1 + \bar{r}) = m_1 p_1$	$w + P_2(1 + \bar{r}) = m_1 P_1$	(2)
$\bar{w} + p_2(1 + \bar{r}) > m'_1 p'_1$	$w + P_2(1 + \bar{r}) = m'_1 P'_1$	(3)
$\bar{w} + p_1(1 + \bar{r}) = q$	$w + P_1(1 + \bar{r}) = q$	(4)
$\bar{w} + p'_1(1 + \bar{r}) > q'$	$w + P'_1(1 + \bar{r}) = q'$	(5)

It may be noted first that, provided (P_1, P_2) is not equal to (p_1, p_2), there will always be a specialisation, using one of the production processes from technique T, which will generate a wage rate greater than the autarky wage rate, $\bar{w}$, this being so whatever the relation between p'_1 and P'_1; hence the existence of the second technique does not affect the argument that, in general, competitive pressures will lead capitalists to specialise and engage in trade whenever that is possible. Furthermore, the four 'negative rules' may be applied as before to those processes of production entering technique T. Indeed, they may also be applied to the component parts of technique T' but it is especially important here to remember that one is dealing only with negative rules: if, for example, $P'_1 > p'_1$, then certainly capitalists will not specialise in the production of C using the M'_1 machine but if $P'_1 < p'_1$ it cannot be said that such a specialisation will be adopted, for $P'_1 < p'_1$ is quite consistent with such a specialisation yielding a wage rate of less than $\bar{w}$ (see (5) above).

While it would be possible to construct a three-dimensional figure, with P_1, P'_1 and P_2 on the axes, which was divided up into regions showing the specialisation adopted at each set of international prices, such a figure would be unduly complicated and could not, in any case, be further generalised to cases with four or more international relative prices. Recourse to the alternative technique of analysis can, however, be made and can lead to an interesting conclusion. The free trade specialisation which maximises the wage rate, and which will thus be the one adopted, may be in a production process that would not be used at all under autarky.

To illustrate this result, assume that $P_1 = p_1, P_2 = p_2, P'_1 < p'_1$. A specialisation in any of the three processes making up technique T would merely yield a wage rate equal to the autarky wage rate, $\bar{w}$, while a specialisation in the production of the M'_1 machine would actually yield a

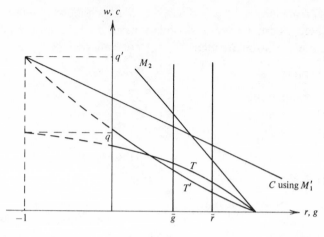

Fig. 8.1

wage rate lower than $\bar{w}$ (see (1) to (4) above). If P'_1 were only marginally less than p'_1, then a specialisation in C production using the M'_1 machine as an input would also yield a wage rate less than $\bar{w}$ but a P'_1 sufficiently less than p'_1 could imply a free trade wage greater than $\bar{w}$; as an extreme case, suppose that $P'_1 = 0$, so that the wage with such a specialisation would be given by $w = q'$. Clearly, if $q' > \bar{w}$, P'_1 can be sufficiently low that the free trade specialisation will be in C production using the M'_1 machine, even though that process would not be used, with $r = \bar{r}$, under autarkic conditions. It may be concluded that, unfortunate as this may be for the trade theorist, one cannot simplify the analysis of the pattern of specialisation by ignoring those production processes which would not be used under autarky.

The existence of a choice of technique in no way alters our earlier finding that the pattern of specialisation adopted under free trade may or may not maximise the level of consumption, per unit of employment, consistent with a given rate of growth, $\bar{g}$. Figure 8.1, drawn for the case $m_1 > m_2 > m'_1$, illustrates both the result, discussed above, that specialisation may be in a process not used under autarky and the possibility that specialisation may be non-optimal in terms of consumption, when $g < r$. Thus it will be seen that the free trade specialisation, at $r = \bar{r}$, will be in the production of C, using the M'_1 machine, and that that specialisation will yield a lower value of c, at $g = \bar{g}$, than would an M_2 specialisation.

Different M_2 machines

Consider now the other kind of choice of technique discussed in chapter 3, part II, in which the one kind of M_1 machine, used in producing C, can be produced by means of two different types of M_2 machine, each of which can also be used in the production of further M_2 machines of the same kind as itself. Defining the alternative techniques by $T \equiv (m_2, m_1, q)$ and and $T'' \equiv (m_2'', m_1'', q)$, the reader may now write down the appropriate autarky and free trade wage–profit relations, under the assumption that, with $r = \bar{r}$, technique T would be adopted under autarky. It is easy to see that, in an obvious notation, there will always be a specialisation, using one of the T processes, which will yield a wage rate higher than the autarky wage rate, whatever the relation between P_2'' and p_2'', provided that (P_1, P_2) is not equal to (p_1, p_2). Again the four negative rules may be applied (with particular attention to their negative nature in the case of M_2'' using processes) and again a three-dimensional diagram, now with P_1, P_2 and P_2'' on the axes, could be divided into different regions of specialisation. Just as above, it may be seen, by means of the alternative technique of analysis, that the free trade specialisation may or may not be in a production process which would be used under autarky and that, as in the absence of a choice of technique, the free trade specialisation may or may not be optimal, in terms of consumption, when $g < r$.

Generalising the above, one might suppose there to be any number of alternative M_1 and M_2 type machines and, indeed, it might be assumed that M_2 machines are made not by themselves but by M_3 machines which can be used in the production of either M_2 or M_3 machines. (Obviously one need not stop even at M_3 machines but can generalise to the case of M_n type machines.) It will still be found that, while the 'negative rules' can be used to rule out many of the logically possible specialisations at any given international prices, many other possible specialisations will still remain to be considered and that the one chosen under free trade conditions may or may not involve the operation of a production process that would be used under autarky. The result that specialisation will always be 'profitable', provided that international relative prices for the commodities which would be produced under autarky differ from the corresponding autarky relative prices, continues to hold, as does the result that nothing can be said *a priori* concerning the consumption optimality or non-optimality of free trade. The existence of a choice of technique does not, of course, affect the general conclusion of chapter 4 that the pattern of free trade specialisation will depend upon international prices, the properties of the available methods of production and the level of the given rate of profit.

MANY COMMODITIES

The existence of many commodities, like that of a choice of technique, means that only rather restricted statements can be made, *a priori*, concerning the free trade pattern of specialisation in a small economy. It can be shown that, provided international relative prices differ from the corresponding autarky prices, there will always be at least one specialisation that will yield a wage rate higher than the autarky wage rate for the given rate of profit and that certain 'negative rules' can be stated showing that certain specialisations will not be adopted when certain relations hold between international and autarky prices. Beyond that, however, little can be added to the assertion that capitalists will adopt the specialisation yielding the highest wage for the given profit rate and international prices.

Suppose, for example, that one were to extend our usual analysis, as suggested in the previous section, by allowing for the existence of n types of machine, where m_j units of the M_j machine are made by one unit of labour working with one M_{j+1} type machine, except when $j = n$, in which case the M_n machines are made by one unit of labour using one M_n machine. Writing down the autarky and free trade relations as usual, one finds that, in an obvious notation;

a C specialisation will not be adopted if $P_1 > p_1$

an M_j „   „ „ „   „   „ $P_j < p_j, P_{j+1} > p_{j+1}$

an M_n „   „ „ „   „   „ $P_n < p_n$

an M_{n-1} „   „ „ „   „   „ $m_{n-1}P_{n-1} < m_nP_n$

an M_n „   „ „ „   „   „ $m_{n-1}P_{n-1} > m_nP_n$

At any given set of international prices, $(P_1, P_2, \ldots, P_n)$, a number of logically possible specialisations will be ruled out by the above 'negative rules' but, in general, further analysis will be required to show which specialisation will be adopted and little of use may be said *a priori*, except that the choice will be determined by $(P_1, \ldots, P_n)$, by the technical coefficients of production $(q, m_1, m_2, \ldots, m_n)$ and by the rate of profit.

Analogous remarks may be made for the case of an arbitrary number of commodities, both consumption commodities and means of production, and an arbitrary number of alternative techniques for the (direct and indirect) production of each consumption commodity. Indeed, attention need no longer be restricted to cases in which production processes use only one produced means of production and produce only one commodity. Let there be n commodities and m processes of production by means of which one unit of labour can, with the aid of specified quantities of the n commodities used as inputs, produce specified quantities of the n commodities as outputs. Which production process will yield the greatest real wage rate for a given rate of profit, i.e. which free trade specialisation will be adopted with that rate of profit, will be determined by the set of international relative prices, by the quantities of commodity inputs to and outputs from each productive process and by the level of the given profit rate, no matter how large m and n may be. There will, furthermore, be no presumption that the specialisation adopted will (or will not) involve a process used under autarky, nor that it will (or will not) be efficient, in terms of consumption per unit of labour, unless the rates of growth and of profit should be equal.

NON-TRADEABLE COMMODITIES

It has been assumed thus far that any commodity is potentially tradeable but such an assumption is obviously not justified. Many services, for example, cannot be exported or imported, trade in certain commodities may be barred by governments for strategic reasons and yet other commodities may not be traded because the transport costs involved would be prohibitive. (From a purely formal point of view, all cases of non-tradeability may be seen as cases of prohibitively, perhaps infinitely, high transport cost.) It is, of course, somewhat inadequate merely to say that certain commodities may be rendered non-tradeable by high transport costs, since those costs ought to be explained within the analysis, but a proper consideration of the productive process of transportation unfortunately lies beyond the scope of the present work. In the following analysis of the effects of non-tradeable commodities, it will therefore be assumed to be known *a priori* which commodities are tradeable and which not.

Taking our basic three commodity model, with no choice of technique, it will be assumed, in turn, that M_2 or M_1 or C is not tradeable. Consideration will then be given to an economy with two tradeable consumption commodities, C and C', and non-tradeable machines, which will be interpreted in terms of the textbook 'Ricardian' model of trade. It will be assumed throughout that the rate of profit is given, as $r = \bar{r}$, and that trade is free from tariffs, etc.; it will be left to the reader to modify the analysis to the case of a given wage rate, to combine the analyses of tariffs and non-traded commodities and to show that, in each case, the consumption–growth frontier continues to be identical to the wage–profit frontier, when trade is balanced.

M_2 non-tradeable

Consider then the (M_2, M_1, C) model of production, under the assumption that the M_2 machine cannot be either exported or imported. In an autarkic economy, for which the non-tradeability of M_2 would naturally make no difference, the following must obtain:

$$\bar{w} + p_1(1 + \bar{r}) = q \tag{6}$$

$$\bar{w} + p_2(1 + \bar{r}) = m_1 p_1 \tag{7}$$

$$\bar{w} + p_2(1 + \bar{r}) = m_2 p_2 \tag{8}$$

In an open economy there are two logically possible patterns of production and trade, given that, as will be assumed throughout, the C commodity has to be made available in the economy (for example, because real wages have to be positive). One possibility is that a C specialisation is adopted, with C being produced and exported, while M_1 machines are imported; if the wage rate yielded by such a specialisation is w^C, then:

$$w^C + P_1(1 + \bar{r}) = q \tag{9}$$

The other possibility is that both M_2 and M_1 machines should be produced, with M_1 machines being exported and the C commodity being imported; if the corresponding wage rate and domestic price of M_2 machines be w^1 and p_2^1 respectively, then:

$$w^1 + p_2^1(1 + \bar{r}) = m_1 P_1 \tag{10}$$

$$w^1 + p_2^1(1 + \bar{r}) = m_2 p_2^1 \tag{11}$$

It will be clear, from (6) and (9), that $w^C \lesseqgtr \bar{w}$ according as $P_1 \gtreqless p_1$. Now it follows from (7), (8), (10) and (11) that $w^1 \gtreqless \bar{w}$ according as $P_1 \gtreqless p_1$. Hence if $P_1 < p_1$ then $w^C > \bar{w} > w^1$, while if $P_1 > p_1$ then $w^1 > \bar{w}$

$> w^C$. (If $P_1 = p_1$ then $w^C = w^1 = \bar{w}$.) Thus if $P_1 < p_1$ a C specialisation will be adopted, while if $P_1 > p_1$ both M_2 and M_1 will be produced, M_1 being exported and C imported.

It will be noted that $P_1 > p_1$ is now a necessary and sufficient condition for the adoption of a C specialisation, whereas it was only a necessary condition when M_2 was assumed to be tradeable. It should also be noted that when $P_1 > p_1$, so that M_2 is produced and hence p_2^1 exists, $p_2^1 = m_1 P_1/m_2 > m_1 p_1/m_2 = p_2$, i.e. that the effect of trade is to make the price of even the non-traded commodity, M_2, different from the corresponding autarky price; international trade influences the relative prices of all commodities and not only of those which are tradeable. Conversely, non-traded commodities play a role in determining the pattern of trade. As was seen above, the pattern of production and trade is determined by the condition $P_1 \gtrless p_1$, and the level of p_1 depends on m_2, the output coefficient for the non-traded commodity M_2, just as much as it does on m_1 and q, the coefficients for the traded commodities. It also depends, of course, on the level of $\bar{r}$, unless $m_1 = m_2$. Thus the non-tradeability of M_2 in no way alters our earlier general conclusion; the pattern of trade is determined by international relative prices, by the conditions of production of all (tradeable and non-tradeable) commodities and by the level of $\bar{r}$.

In the case of a C specialisation, the wage–profit frontier is simply $w^C = [q - P_1(1 + \bar{r})]$, as it was when M_2 was assumed to be tradeable. The other case, however, implies a wage–profit frontier different from any found in our earlier analysis; by eliminating p_2^1 from (10) and (11) one finds that $w^1 = (m_1 P_1/m_2)[m_2 - (1 + \bar{r})]$. While this frontier is linear, even though two commodities are being produced, it will be seen below that such a result does not hold generally. The reader may now show that, with balanced trade, the consumption–growth frontiers are the same as the corresponding wage–profit frontiers and that the existence of a non-tradeable commodity does not affect the earlier finding that the free trade specialisation may or may not be optimal for consumption (unless $g = r$).

M_1 non-tradeable

Suppose now that the M_1 type machine cannot be either exported or imported; there are again two possibilities. One is that M_2 machines should be produced and exported, while C is imported, i.e. that an M_2

specialisation should be adopted. The corresponding wage rate w^2 must satisfy

$$w^2 + P_2(1 + \bar{r}) = m_2 P_2 \tag{12}$$

The other possibility is that M_1 and C should both be produced, C being exported and M_2 machines, for use in the production of M_1 machines, being imported. If the corresponding wage rate is w^C and the domestic price of M_1 machines is p_1^C then:

$$w^C + p_1^C(1 + \bar{r}) = q \tag{13}$$

$$w^C + P_2(1 + \bar{r}) = m_1 p_1^C \tag{14}$$

It will be clear, from (8) and (12), that $w^2 \gtreqless \bar{w}$ according as $P_2 \gtreqless p_2$ and, from (6) and (13), that $w^C \gtreqless \bar{w}$ according as $p_1^C \lesseqgtr p_1$. Now it follows from (6), (7), (13) and (14) that $p_1^C \lesseqgtr p_1$ according as $P_2 \lesseqgtr p_2$. Hence if $P_2 > p_2$, then $w^2 > \bar{w} > w^C$, while if $P_2 < p_2$ then $w^C > \bar{w} > w^2$. (If $P_2 = p_2$ then $w^C = w^2 = \bar{w}$.) It follows that if $P_2 > p_2$ an M_2 specialisation will be adopted, while if $P_2 < p_2$ both C and M_1 will be produced, with C being exported and M_2 imported.

The above analysis confirms the general results obtained from the previous case. $P_2 > p_2$ is now a necessary and sufficient condition for an M_2 specialisation whereas it was only a necessary condition with all commodities tradeable. Again, in the case of M_1 being produced, its price is different from the corresponding autarky price since, as noted above, $p_1^C < p_1$. (Indeed, as follows from (13) and (14), $p_1^C = [q + P_2(1 + \bar{r})]/[m_1 + (1 + \bar{r})]$, so that p_1^C depends on the profit rate, $\bar{r}$, as well as on P_2, by contrast with the finding above that $p_2^1 (= m_1 P_1/m_2)$ is independent of $\bar{r}$.) As before, the technical conditions of production of the non-traded commodity, represented here by m_1, influence the pattern of trade just as much as those of the other commodities, since that pattern depends on $P_2 \lesseqgtr p_2$ and p_2 depends on m_1.

In the case of an M_2 specialisation the wage–profit frontier will, of course, be given by $w^2 = P_2[m_2 - (1 + \bar{r})]$, as usual. In the other case, however, the frontier is found, on eliminating p_1^C from (13) and (14), to be given by $w^C = [m_1 q - P_2(1 + \bar{r})^2]/[m_1 + (1 + \bar{r})]$; the with-trade wage–profit frontier is no longer linear. The reader may derive the usual results concerning the consumption–growth frontier, with balanced trade, and the consumption optimality or non-optimality of free trade.

C non-tradeable

If the consumption commodity, C, cannot be imported then it must necessarily be produced domestically, which implies, in turn, that M_1 machines must either be imported or produced domestically. There are again just two possibilities. One is that both C and M_1 should be produced domestically, some of the M_1 machines being exported and M_2 machines imported. The other possibility is that both C and M_2 should be produced, some of the M_2 machines being exported and M_1 machines imported. It will be noted that, by contrast with the two cases discussed above, there is now no possibility of a complete specialisation.

In analysing the present case one is faced with the slight difficulty that, there being no world market in C, the international prices of machines in terms of C, P_1 and P_2, are no longer defined. It is therefore necessary to change our normal practice of taking C to be the standard of value; in this section alone, M_1 machines will be taken as the standard of value and the reader must keep constantly in mind the fact that, in this section, the symbols for wage rates and prices do not have their usual meaning.

Taking M_1 machines as the standard of value, the autarky equations will be, in an obvious notation:

$$\bar{w} + (1 + \bar{r}) = qp_c \tag{15}$$

$$\bar{w} + p_2(1 + \bar{r}) = m_1 \tag{16}$$

$$\bar{w} + p_2(1 + \bar{r}) = m_2 p_2 \tag{17}$$

Now, with the same value standard, let the wage rate and the domestic price of C be w^1 and p_c^1 when M_1 is produced and exported but w^2 and p_c^2 when M_2 is produced and exported. Then, if P_2 is the international price of M_2 machines in terms of M_1 machines:

$$w^1 + (1 + \bar{r}) = qp_c^1 \tag{18}$$

$$w^1 + P_2(1 + \bar{r}) = m_1 \tag{19}$$

$$w^2 + (1 + \bar{r}) = qp_c^2 \tag{20}$$

$$w^2 + P_2(1 + \bar{r}) = m_2 P_2 \tag{21}$$

It will be clear, from (16), (17), (19) and (21), that if $P_2 < p_2$ then $w^1 > \bar{w} > w^2$, while if $P_2 > p_2$ then $w^2 > \bar{w} > w^1$. These wage rates, it must be remembered, are wage rates in terms of M_1 machines, not wage rates in terms of C, but it is not difficult to show that the latter wage rates will be ordered in the same way as the 'M_1' wage rates. It may be concluded that if $P_2 < p_2$ then C and M_1 will be produced, with M_1 exported and M_2 imported, while if $P_2 > p_2$, C and M_2 will be produced, with M_2 exported and M_1 imported; M_1 or M_2 will be produced and exported according as the international price of M_2, in terms of M_1, is less than or greater than the corresponding autarky price.

It may be noted that, with C non-tradeable, a necessary and sufficient condition for the export of $M_2(M_1)$ is that the international price of M_2 in terms of M_1 (of M_1 in terms of M_2) should exceed the corresponding autarky price, whereas that is only a necessary condition when C is tradeable. It may be noted also that, as may be seen from (15), (18) and (20), the domestic price of C will differ from the autarky price p_c, with $p_c^1 > p_c$ when M_1 is exported and $p_c^2 > p_c$ when M_2 is exported; in each case the with-trade value of the non-tradeable C commodity is higher, relative to its means of production M_1, than it would be under autarky, so that, again, trade is found to affect the relative price of a non-traded commodity. By contrast with the above cases of M_2 or M_1 being non-tradeable, however, the conditions of production of the non-tradeable commodity C, represented by q, now play no role in determining the pattern of trade. That pattern is determined by $P_2 \lessgtr p_2 = (m_1/m_2)$, so that neither q nor $\bar{r}$ influences the pattern of trade; as will be seen below, the level of productivity in C production will simply affect the level of the real wage corresponding to any given $\bar{r}$. In the present case, then, the pattern of trade is determined solely by international relative prices and the conditions of production of the tradeable commodities; though it must be remembered that it is the existence of and need for the non-traded C commodity which prevents complete specialisation in production, so that the presence of C affects the pattern of output even though it does not affect the pattern of trade.

From (18) and (19), or from (20) and (21), it will be found that the wage rates, in terms of C, for the alternative patterns of trade are given by

$$(w^1/p_c^1) = q\left[\frac{m_1 - P_2(1 + \bar{r})}{m_1 + (1 - P_2)(1 + \bar{r})}\right]$$

$$(w^2/p_c^2) = q\left\{\frac{P_2[m_2 - (1 + \bar{r})]}{m_2 P_2 + (1 - P_2)(1 + \bar{r})}\right\}$$

It will be seen that each of these with-trade wage–profit frontiers is non-linear (unless $P_2 = 1$, i.e. unless one M_2 machine exchanges for one M_1 machine on the world market). The reader may now derive the two appropriate consumption–growth frontiers, show that the free trade specialisation may or may not be optimal for consumption (when $g \neq r$) and should then recall that henceforth the C commodity will again be taken as the standard of value.

A number of general conclusions emerge from the analysis of the above three cases. The existence of non-traded commodities does not remove the 'motive to trade', since trade will still be 'profitable' provided that international relative prices of the tradeable commodities differ from the corresponding autarky prices. Complete specialisation in production may or may not occur, however. Furthermore, just as the presence of trade will, in general, cause the prices of non-traded commodities to differ from the corresponding autarky prices, so the presence of non-traded commodities will, in general, play a role in determining the pattern of production and the pattern of trade. Thus it may still be said that the pattern of production and trade in a small economy will be determined by international relative prices, the available methods of production and the rate of profit, even in the presence of non-traded commodities.

Trade in consumption commodities alone

Consider now economies of a kind discussed in chapter 3, part II, in which there are two different consumption commodities, C and C', which are produced by labour working with M_1 and M_1' machines respectively, the latter being produced with the aid of a common M_2 machine, which can also be used in making M_2 machines. If it is assumed that the consumption commodities are tradeable but that the various machines are not, then one can construct a model of trade in consumption commodities alone; such a model of trade is, strangely, common in textbooks, where it is often described as 'Ricardian'.

Taking the C commodity as the standard of value and adopting the notation used in chapter 3, part II, the following must hold in an autarkic economy in which both C and C' are produced:

$$\bar{w} + p_2(1 + \bar{r}) = m_2 p_2 \tag{22}$$

$$\bar{w} + p_2(1 + \bar{r}) = m_1 p_1 \tag{23}$$

$$\bar{w} + p_2(1 + \bar{r}) = m_1' p_1' \tag{24}$$

$$\bar{w} + p_1(1 + \bar{r}) = q \tag{25}$$

$$\bar{w} + p_1'(1 + \bar{r}) = q' p_c' \tag{26}$$

Suppose now that the international price of C', in terms of C, is P'_c, where $P'_c < p'_c$, and consider an open economy in which M_2, M_1 and C are produced but M'_1 and C' are not; C is exported and C' is imported. Relations (22), (23) and (25) will hold in such an open economy, just as in an autarkic one, and hence, with $r = \bar{r}$ in both economies, the autarky values of the wage rate and the prices of the M_1 and M_2 machines will also rule in the open economy. With a given wage in terms of C, however, workers in the open economy have a higher wage than those in the autarkic economy in terms of C', since $P'_c < p'_c$, and thus, provided that C' enters the consumption of workers, the 'real wage' will be higher in the open economy than in the autarkic one. In the same way, the prices of the M_2 and M_1 machines in terms of C' will be higher in the open economy than in the autarkic one, so that it can again be said that trade influences relative prices of the non-traded commodities. If $P'_c > p'_c$, then the whole argument can, of course, be repeated with M'_1 and C' in place of M_1 and C respectively; with C' exported and C imported, the wage rate and the prices of the M_2 and M'_1 machines, in terms of C', will be the same in the open and the autarkic economies but they will all be higher in the open economy in terms of C. Thus trade will affect the relative prices of non-traded commodities and will yielded a 'real wage' greater than the autarky one, provided that C enters the workers' consumption bundle.

The pattern of trade is thus determined, in the present case, by the condition $P'_c \lesseqgtr p'_c$. Now it is commonly said in the textbooks that, in 'Ricardian' models of trade in consumption commodities, the pattern of trade is determined by technical conditions of production alone. It was shown in chapter 3, part II, however, that the general expression for p'_c is

$$p'_c = \left[\frac{m_1 q}{m'_1 q'} \right] \left[\frac{m'_1 m_2 + (m_2 - m'_1)(1 + \bar{r})}{m_1 m_2 + (m_2 - m_1)(1 + \bar{r})} \right]$$

If $m'_1 = m_1$, then $p'_c = (q/q')$ and is indeed determined by technical conditions alone. In the general case, however, p'_c depends both on technical conditions (represented by m_2, m_1, m'_1, q and q') and on the given rate of profit, $\bar{r}$. Thus the pattern of trade implied, in this model, by a given international price ratio P'_c, will depend on the level of $\bar{r}$, unless P'_c should be either smaller than the lowest possible value of p'_c or greater than the highest possible value of p'_c. (Suppose, for example, that $m_2 = m_1 = 2$, $m'_1 = 1$ and $q = q' = 6$; it follows that, in an autarkic economy, $p'_c = 0.5$ $(3 + \bar{r})$. Since $\bar{r}$ might lie anywhere in the range $0 \leq \bar{r} \leq (m_2 - 1) = 1$, p'_c can lie anywhere in the range $1.5 \leq p'_c \leq 2$. Then, if $1.5 < P'_c < 2$, the

pattern of trade will depend on the level of the given rate of profit, $\bar{r}$.)
Hence it has again been found that the pattern of trade will be determined
by international prices, by the conditions of production of both tradeable
and non-tradeable commodities and by the level of $\bar{r}$.

That the free trade specialisation can be inefficient, in terms of consumption per unit of employment, can also be seen in the present kind of model;
the numerical example of the previous paragraph will be used as an
illustration. It will be convenient to assume here, by contrast with the
rest of this chapter, that the real wage is now given, as an exogenously
determined bundle of C and C' per unit of labour, say $(\bar{w}, \bar{w}')$. It will also be
assumed, for simplicity, that capitalists do not save, so that $g = s = 0$.
Consider Fig. 8.2, in which c is consumption of C per unit of employment,
c' is consumption of C' per unit of employment, and XY shows the
combinations of C and C' consumption available in an autarkic economy,
per unit of employment, when the rate of growth is zero. The slope of XY
is 1.5 because that is what p'_c would be if $\bar{r}$ were zero; assuming that $\bar{r}$ is
positive, however, it follows that $p'_c > 1.5$, as in Fig. 8.2.

Suppose now that $1.5 < P'_c < p'_c$. Capitalists will be led to produce and
export C but to import, rather than produce, C', so that the possible
available bundles of consumption, per unit of employment, will lie on XZ
in Fig. 8.2. It will be seen that, point X apart, XZ lies wholly inside XY,
so that as between two economies with the same available methods of
production and the same (zero) rate of growth, the open economy has a

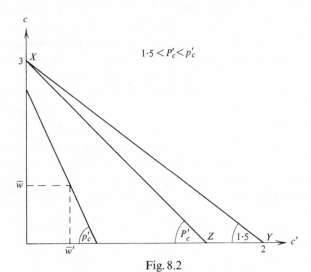

Fig. 8.2

more restricted set of consumption possibilities than has the autarkic economy.

SUMMARY

It has been shown that the analysis presented in chapters 4 and 5 is not quite as restrictive as it might have appeared. Once the basic principles have been established, certain complications—such as the existence of a choice of technique, or of a multiplicity of commodities or of non-tradeable commodities—can readily be introduced, without causing any major modification to the general conclusions previously obtained.

Thus it has been seen that the introduction of either a choice of technique or a multiplicity of commodities leaves unchanged the results that (i) international prices different from autarky prices will induce capitalists to specialise in production and to trade, (ii) the (proximate) determinants of the pattern of specialisation are the set of international prices, the exogenously given profit rate (or wage rate) and the properties of the available methods of production and (iii) the free trade specialisation can yield a positive, a zero or a negative 'gain from trade'. It was noted that a free trade specialisation might or might not involve the use of a productive process that would be used under autarky.

Again, it has been seen that the introduction of non-tradeable commodities into the analysis leaves unaffected the propositions (i), (ii) and (iii) set out in the preceding paragraph (subject to a slight qualification being necessary to proposition (ii) when the consumption commodity is non-tradeable). It was noted that, in the presence of non-tradeables, specialisation may or may not be complete (except in the non-tradeable consumption commodity case), that (in general) the production conditions of *all* commodities, tradeable and non-tradeable, play a role in determining the pattern of specialisation and that trade affects the domestic relative prices of *all* commodities, tradeables and non-tradeables. (It was also remarked that, contrary to many 'textbook' treatments, the pattern of trade, when the only tradeables are two consumption commodities, is *not* determined by international prices and production conditions alone and that such trade can yield a positive, a zero or a negative 'gain from trade'.)

9
A SIMPLE ANALYSIS OF INTERNATIONAL EQUILIBRIUM

Thus far, attention has been directed to the analysis of a single economy, whose capitalists face given international prices and can, under free trade, export or import any quantity of any commodity at those prices. No attention has been given to the questions how international prices are determined and how the production and trading decisions of capitalists in different countries can be consistent. The purpose of this chapter is to answer these two (closely related) questions, albeit in a very simple context.

It will be assumed that there are just two countries, named Xeres and Zend, in the world economy and that there are only three commodities, the C, M_1 and M_2 commodities discussed above. All three commodities will be taken to be tradeable on fully competitive world markets, trade being free from any transport costs, tariffs, quotas, taxes, etc. ... (That there are only two countries is quite consistent with world markets being competitive, it should be remembered, provided that the number of competing capitalists in each country is large.) While all commodities will be assumed to be internationally mobile, including the capital goods M_1 and M_2, money capital will be assumed not to flow between countries, so that no tendency toward an international uniformity of profit rates will be assumed. (Such an assumption is not, of course, entirely realistic under the conditions of modern capitalism but it is justified here on the grounds that it would not be sensible to relax it without entering into a full analysis of the inter-relationships between international trade and international investment, which is not possible in the present work.) Labour will also be assumed not to move between countries.

Each country will be assumed to have access to just one process of production for the production of each of the three commodities, there being no 'choice of technique' in either country. In general, however, it will not be assumed that the available process of production for a given commodity is the same in both countries; inter-country differences in natural conditions, in scientific and technological experience and in industrial conditions of skill, labour discipline, etc., would make such an assumption highly implausible. Since the highly convenient assumption that one unit of labour always works with one machine will, nevertheless, be retained, the properties of the available productive processes in the countries Xeres and Zend may be represented by (q^X, m_1^X, m_2^X) and (q^Z, m_1^Z, m_2^Z) respectively.

As was noted in chapter 3, the analysis of growth in a closed economy can be made reasonably simple only under the rather drastic assumption that all outputs and quantities of labour employed grow at the same, constant rate, i.e. that there is steady, or 'quasi-stationary', growth. For the most part, the following analysis of growing, trading economies will, unfortunately, have to be carried out under that same assumption, the uniform and constant rate of steady growth now being uniform not only for those output and labour quantities relating to a given country but also as between countries. (If the two countries were to grow at different rates then, with complete or partial specialisation by both countries, international prices would change through time, so that capitalists' expectations would have to be analysed explicitly—doubtless under assumptions no less implausible than the assumption of equal, steady growth rates.)

On the basis of the assumptions set out above, it will now be considered whether there exists a set of international prices (P_1, P_2) such that the patterns of production and trade, freely chosen by the capitalists of Xeres and Zend, will be mutually consistent with one another and with the maintenance of steady growth at a rate g, and such that the profit rate in each country satisfies the relation $s^i r^i = g, (i = X, Z)$; it will be considered, that is, whether an international equilibrium exists. As usual, however, we shall not approach the main question directly but rather via a number of intermediate steps.

EQUILIBRIUM INTERNATIONAL PRICES

As a preliminary step towards the actual determination of equilibrium international prices, it will be useful to note four conditions which must be satisfied by any such prices, for the simultaneous application of the four conditions will serve to show immediately that many pairs of international prices (P_1, P_2) cannot possibly be equilibrium prices. The first condition springs from the fact that with three commodities and only two countries—and all three commodities must be produced if any C is to be produced—it is not possible for both countries to be completely specialised. It follows at once that equilibrium international prices must lie on a line of semi-specialisation for at least one of the countries.

The other three conditions arise from the application to the present situation of the 'negative rules' set out in chapter 4. It was shown there, for example, that capitalists would not produce C if $P_1 > p_1$; thus if C has to be produced in Xeres and/or Zend, as will be assumed throughout, it follows that P_1 must not exceed the greater of p_1^X, p_1^Z (where p_1^i is the p_1 for country i). Again, as was shown in chapter 4, capitalists will not produce M_2 machines if $P_2 < p_2$ which, in the present context, means that an equilibrium value of P_2 cannot be less than the smaller of p_2^X, p_2^Z.

To derive the fourth condition, suppose that the countries have been named in such a way that $(m_1^X/m_2^X) > (m_1^Z/m_2^Z)$. Now if the international prices (P_1, P_2) were such that $(P_2/P_1) > (m_1^X/m_2^X)$, then the relation $m_2 P_2 > m_1 P_1$ would apply in both countries and thus, as shown in chapter 4, capitalists in neither country would produce M_1 machines. On the other hand, if prices were such that $(m_1^Z/m_2^Z) > (P_2/P_1)$, then the relation $m_1 P_1 > m_2 P_2$ would hold in both countries and thus, as shown in chapter 4, neither set of capitalists would produce M_2 machines. Hence, if (P_1, P_2) are to be equilibrium international prices they must satisfy the condition $(m_1^X/m_2^X) \geq (P_2/P_1) \geq (m_1^Z/m_2^Z)$. This last condition can, of course, be rewritten in terms of autarky prices, as $(p_2^X/p_1^X) \geq (P_2/P_1) \geq (p_2^Z/p_1^Z)$; the relative price of M_1 and M_2 machines, in an international equilibrium, must lie between the two corresponding autarky price ratios.

Thus if (P_1, P_2) are to be equilibrium international prices, they must satisfy the following four conditions:

Condition 1: (P_1, P_2) must lie on a line of semi-specialisation for at least one of the countries
Condition 2: P_1 must not exceed the greater of p_1^X, p_1^Z
Condition 3: P_2 must be not less than the smaller of p_2^X, p_2^Z
Condition 4: (P_2/P_1) must be neither greater than the greater of, nor smaller than the smaller of (p_2^X/p_1^X) and (p_2^Z/p_1^Z)

These four conditions taken together, while they do not determine equilibrium international prices, do severely restrict the pairs of international prices which need to be considered as possible equilibrium prices.

COMPARATIVE ADVANTAGE

It was seen in chapter 4 how the set of non-negative international prices can, for a single country, be divided into three regions showing which specialisation, or semi-specialisation, will be adopted, under free trade conditions, at any given (P_1, P_2); the positions and shapes of the lines separating the three regions were seen to depend on the technical conditions of production and on the level of the autonomously determined wage rate or rate of profit. Now this procedure may be adopted for Xeres and Zend in turn, the two sets of lines of semi-specialisation being drawn on the same diagram. With the countries so named that $(m_1^X/m_2^X) > (m_1^Z/m_2^Z)$ and with the assumption that the two profit rates are given as $\bar{r}^X$ and $\bar{r}^Z$, the various possible relative positions of the two sets of semi-specialisation lines will be as shown in Fig. 9.1, where the solid lines refer to Xeres and the broken ones to Zend, while points X and Z mark the autarky price points for Xeres and Zend respectively. (It will be clear that two other, rather marginal, cases exist in which a line of semi-specialisation for one country passes through the autarky price point for the other; these singular cases will be ignored.) The resulting figure would be little different if the wage rate, rather than the rate of profit, were assumed to be given in one or both of the countries, the only modification being, of course, that the corresponding CM_1 and CM_2 lines of semi-specialisation would no longer be linear (see chapter 4). Reference will therefore be made to Fig. 9.1 even in cases where the profit rate is not taken to be given in both countries, for it would be superfluous to redraw Fig. 9.1 for each possible combination of exogenously given wage or profit rates, when the reader can mentally 'bend' the CM_1 and CM_2 lines of Fig. 9.1 as required.

Now, in Figs. 9.1(a)–(c), consider the international prices (P_1, P_2) lying on either XY or YZ; reflection will show that any such prices not only satisfy the four conditions set out above but do, indeed, ensure that each of

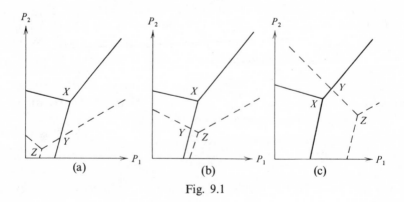

Fig. 9.1

the three commodities may be produced in at least one of the two countries (in exactly one of the two countries if the end-points X, Y and Z are ignored). The reader must now study Fig. 9.1 until satisfied that no other international prices have those properties. No matter which of the Figs. 9.1 obtains, only the prices (P_1, P_2) which lie on either XY or YZ are possible equilibrium prices. Since the conditions of production and the exogenously given wage and/or profit rates suffice to determine which of Figs. 9.1 applies and to define the corresponding lines XY and YZ, it may be said that the production conditions and the exogenously determined distributive variables suffice to restrict closely, though not to determine, the equilibrium international prices.

The conclusions reached so far all relate to international prices; some remarks may now be made concerning the pattern of production and trade in an international equilibrium. Scrutiny of Figs. 9.1(a)–(c) will quickly reveal that whenever the equilibrium international price ratio for machines lies *strictly* between the corresponding autarky price ratios—i.e. when (P_1, P_2) lies *strictly* between X and Y in Fig. 9.1(a), X and Z in Fig. 9.1(b) or Y and Z in Fig. 9.1(c)—M_1 machines are produced only in Xeres, while M_2 machines are produced only in Zend. Now the condition $(m_1^X/m_2^X) > (m_1^Z/m_2^Z)$ may be interpreted as stating that, with respect to machine production and leaving aside the matter of C production, M_1 production is carried out *relatively* more efficiently in Xeres, while M_2 production is carried out *relatively* more efficiently in Zend. (Some readers may find this interpretation more obvious if the condition is rewritten as $(m_1^X/m_1^Z) > (m_2^X/m_2^Z)$.) In the traditional terminology of trade theory, that is, Xeres may be said to have a comparative advantage in the production of M_1 machines and Zend to have a comparative advantage in the production of M_2 machines; the force of the adjective 'comparative' is, of course, that only the 'relative' efficiencies of production are involved, no reference being necessary to the 'absolute' advantages indicated by the conditions $m_1^X \gtrless m_1^Z, m_2^X \gtrless m_2^Z$.

Using this terminology, it may thus be said that whenever equilibrium international prices are such that (P_2/P_1) lies strictly between the corresponding autarky price ratios, each type of machine will be produced only in the country having a comparative advantage in the production of that machine. When both machines are traded, furthermore, it can be said that each type of machine will be exported from the country having a comparative advantage in its production. It must be noted, however, that the result concerning the location of production is of more general application than that concerning the pattern of machine exports; if equilibrium international prices should lie on XY in Fig. 9.1(a) or Fig. 9.1(b), both C and M_1 will be produced exclusively in Xeres and thus M_1 machines will not be traded. It must also be noted that even the location of production result fails to apply if (P_2/P_1), rather than lying strictly between (p_2^X/p_1^X) and (p_2^Z/p_1^Z), should be equal to one of those ratios: for if equilibrium international prices should lie on YZ in Fig. 9.1(a), or on XY in Fig. 9.1(c), then both machines will be produced in the same country. M_2 machines will not be traded in this case, so that it is seen again that, while both M_1 and M_2 machines are *tradeable*, one of them may not be *traded* in international equilibrium.

TWO SPECIAL CASES

In Fig. 9.1 the only restriction that is placed on the technical conditions of production in Xeres and Zend is that $(m_1^X/m_2^X) > (m_1^Z/m_2^Z)$; in the present section two special cases will be considered, the first of which will serve to provide further illustration of the concept of comparative advantage, while the second will highlight the role of the exogenously determined distributive variables in the determination of the equilibrium pattern of production and trade. In the first case, technical conditions of production which make autarky prices quite independent of distribution will be assumed, so that distribution considerations play no role; while in the second case technical conditions will be assumed to be identical as between Xeres and Zend, so that no technical comparative advantage considerations can arise.

Suppose first, then, that $m_1^X = m_2^X = m^X$ and that $m_1^Z = m_2^Z = m^Z$; in each country autarky prices will be determined, by the technical conditions alone, as $p_1^X = p_2^X = (q^X/m^X)$ and $p_1^Z = p_2^Z = (q^Z/m^Z)$. Let absolute efficiency be greater in Xeres in all lines of production, so that $q^X > q^Z$ and $m^X > m^Z$ and suppose that Xeres has the *comparative* advantage in C production, while Zend has the *comparative* advantage in machine production, i.e. that $(q^X/m^X) > (q^Z/m^Z)$. In this—very special—case, Fig. 9.1 will collapse to Fig. 9.2. Now reflection will show that if (P_1, P_2) are to be equilibrium international prices, they must lie on XZ in Fig. 9.2; (P_1, P_2) must lie on the 45° line through the origin if both M_1 and M_2 machines are to be produced and cannot lie below Z—for capitalists in both countries would then wish to produce only C—nor above X—for capitalists in neither country would then wish to produce C. With international prices lying between X

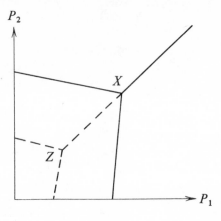

Fig. 9.2

and Z, it will be seen that capitalists in Xeres will produce and export the consumption commodity C, while capitalists in Zend will produce M_1 and M_2 machines, exporting only the M_1 machines, of course. Thus both C and the machines will be produced in the country having the comparative advantage in their production and the exports of C and M_1 will each be from the country having the appropriate comparative advantage.

By contrast with the previous case, suppose now that production conditions are the same in both countries ($q^X = q^Z = q, m_1^X = m_1^Z = m_1, m_2^X = m_2^Z = m_2$) so that, *ex hypothesi*, the pattern of production and trade cannot be explained in terms of technical comparative advantage. If $m_1 \neq m_2$ then, as was seen in chapter 3, autarky prices will differ as between Xeres and Zend, unless the two countries should have the same autarky wage and profit rates. Thus suppose, for example, that Xeres and Zend have exogenously determined profit rates $\bar{r}^X$ and $\bar{r}^Z$ such that $\bar{r}^X > \bar{r}^Z$; Fig. 9.1 will now become Figs. 9.3(a), (b), which simply reproduce Figs. 4.4(a), (c). In each case, only prices lying on XZ are possible equilibrium international prices, with the capitalists in one country producing and exporting C and those in the other country producing both M_1 and M_2 machines and exporting the former. Given that $\bar{r}^X > \bar{r}^Z$, however, the pattern of production and trade depends on whether $m_1 > m_2$ or $m_2 > m_1$; and, as the reader may check, for either relative magnitude of m_1 and m_2, the pattern would be reversed if $\bar{r}^X$ were smaller rather than greater than $\bar{r}^Z$. Thus trade can occur between countries with identical conditions of production, the pattern of production and trade being dependent on the magnitudes of the given rates of profit (or, of course, given wage rates).

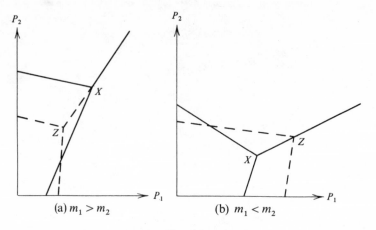

Fig. 9.3

It has been seen that in each of the above special cases, equilibrium international prices (P_1, P_2) must be such that both P_1 and P_2 lie between the corresponding autarky prices; in the first case, for example, $p_1^z < P_1 < p_1^x$ and $p_2^z < P_2 < p_2^x$. It should be noted carefully, therefore, that this result does *not* hold generally; while it does hold in Fig. 9.1(a), it does *not* do so for (P_1, P_2) on XY in either Fig. 9.1(b) or Fig. 9.1(c), for example.

WAGES, PROFITS AND PRICES

The above preliminary analysis has been carried out in terms of diagrams, such as Fig. 9.1, in which the principal emphasis has been on the role of international prices. It will now be useful to direct attention more explicitly to the way in which wage rates and/or profit rates in the world economy depend on international prices and on one another.

Suppose, for example, that Fig. 9.1(a) applies, so that international prices must, if they are to be possible equilibrium prices, lie on XY or YZ. If (P_1, P_2) lie on XY, then C and M_1 are produced in Xeres and M_2 in Zend so that the following relations must hold:

$$w^X + P_1(1 + r^X) = q^X \tag{1}$$

$$w^X + P_2(1 + r^X) = m_1^X P_1 \tag{2}$$

$$w^Z + P_2(1 + r^Z) = m_2^Z P_2 \tag{3}$$

If, on the other hand, (P_1, P_2) lie on YZ, then C and M_2 are still produced in Xeres and Zend respectively but M_1 machines are now produced in Zend; hence (1) and (3) still apply but (2) is replaced by:

$$w^Z + P_2(1 + r^Z) = m_1^Z P_1 \tag{4}$$

Now consider the alternative pairs of international prices (P_1, P_2) lying on XYZ; the further along XYZ is the point considered, the lower are both P_1 and P_2. It will be seen from (1) that the lower is P_1, the higher is the with-trade wage–profit frontier in Xeres and from (3) that the lower is P_2, the lower is the with-trade wage–profit frontier in Zend. Hence the wage–profit frontier is higher for Xeres and lower for Zend as one considers points further and further along XYZ; at X itself, of course, (P_1, P_2) $= (p_1^X, p_2^X)$ and the Xeres frontier is its autarky frontier, while at the other extreme, Z, $(P_1, P_2) = (p_1^Z, p_2^Z)$ and thus Zend's frontier is now its autarky frontier. The heights of the two countries' wage–profit frontiers are thus inversely related, as one considers alternative (P_1, P_2), in addition to the wage and profit rates in a given country being inversely related to one another, for given (P_1, P_2). It can thus be concluded that each of the four distributive variables w^X, r^X, w^Z, r^Z is inversely related to each of the other three and that to each possible combination of those variables there corresponds a particular pair of international prices (P_1, P_2).

It may be helpful to repeat the above argument rather more formally. Suppose first that (P_1, P_2) lie on XY so that (1), (2) and (3) hold. To show how the wage and profit rates can vary as (P_1, P_2) vary, it is necessary to eliminate P_1 and P_2 from (1), (2) and (3). One then obtains the 'international wage–profit frontier':

$$(m_1^X + 1 + r^X)w^X + \left[\frac{(1 + r^X)^2}{m_2^Z - (1 + r^Z)}\right]w^Z = m_1^X q^X \tag{5}$$

In the same way, if (P_1, P_2) lie on YZ then, on eliminating P_1 and P_2 from (1), (3) and (4), one obtains another such frontier:

$$m_1^Z[m_2^Z - (1 + r^Z)]w^X + m_2^Z(1 + r^X)w^Z = m_1^Z q^X[m_2^Z - (1 + r^Z)] \tag{6}$$

Given rates of profit

These rather fearsome equations can be rendered somewhat less forbidding by considering first the case in which r^X and r^Z are both given, as $\bar{r}^X$ and $\bar{r}^Z$ respectively. With both r^X and r^Z thus turned into constants, it will be seen that (5) and (6) are both simple linear relations between w^X and w^Z

and that, in each case, w^X and w^Z are inversely related; neither wage rate can be increased except at the expense of the other. To any given pair (w^X, w^Z) satisfying either (5) or (6), there corresponds, it must not be forgotten, a particular pair of international prices (P_1, P_2), which can be found from (1) and (3).

Continuing the analysis of the case of given profit rates, $\bar{r}^X$ and $\bar{r}^Z$, the linear w^X/w^Z frontiers given by (5) and (6) may be drawn on the same diagram as in Fig. 9.4, which should be considered in conjunction with Fig. 9.1(a). If international prices lie at point X in Fig. 9.1(a), then w^X and w^Z will lie at point x in Fig. 9.4, with w^X naturally being equal to the autarky wage $\bar{w}^X$. For prices lying between X and Y in Fig. 9.1(a), the wage rates w^X and w^Z will lie at a corresponding point on xy in Fig. 9.4. With prices at Y in Fig. 9.1(a), M_1 machines might be produced in Xeres and/or Zend but, wherever the production of M_1 machines is located, the wage rates w^X and w^Z will necessarily lie at point y in Fig. 9.4. Finally, if prices lie between Y and Z in Fig. 9.1(a), then the wage rates will lie at a corresponding point between y and z in Fig. 9.4, while if prices are at point Z in Fig. 9.1(a), the wage rates will be at z in Fig. 9.4, with w^Z taking its autarky level, $\bar{w}^Z$.

The general case

Returning to (5) and (6) and dropping the assumption that r^X and r^Z are given, it is not difficult to show that if (w^X, w^Z) or (w^X, r^Z) or (r^X, w^Z) or (r^X, r^Z) are taken to be at given levels, then (5) and (6) both define an inverse

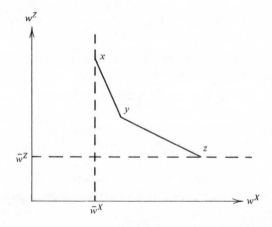

Fig. 9.4

relationship between the remaining two variables and that corresponding xy and yz frontiers may be drawn up, much as in Fig. 9.4. In each case, of course, the variable relating to Xeres will take its autarky value when prices lie at X in Fig. 9.1(a), while that relating to Zend will do likewise when prices lie at Z in Fig. 9.1(a). It should be noted that the frontiers xy and yz will not necessarily be linear; for example if one sets $w^X = \bar{w}^X$ and $w^Z = \bar{w}^Z$ in (5) and (6), under the assumption that wage rates are exogenously determined, then (6) will define a linear, inverse relation between r^X and r^Z but (5) will define a non-linear, inverse relation between them. Whether they be linear or not, however, there will always be well-defined, downward sloping xy and yz frontiers, showing an inverse relation between the wage and/or profit rates that are not exogenously determined, each point on those frontiers being associated with a particular pair of international prices (P_1, P_2). The precise positions of the frontiers will, of course, in each case depend on the values of the technical production coefficients (the qs and the ms) and of the exogenously given wage and/or profit rates. Other things being equal, a frontier will be 'further out' from the origin the higher the value of any relevant q or m coefficient—i.e. the more efficient is any relevant production process—and the lower is either of the exogenously given wage or profit rates.

Leaving the reader to check carefully that the argument of this section has been fully grasped and that it needs little modification to be applied to the cases of Fig. 9.1(b) and Fig. 9.1(c), we may at last turn to some examples of the determination of international equilibrium. It is to be noted carefully that that determination will be carried out in stages. In the immediately following sections, attention will be focussed on the wage rates, the profit and growth rates, the prices and the *pattern* of production and trade obtaining in an international equilibrium and, indeed, 'equilibrium' is there to be understood in this qualified sense. In a subsequent section (pp. 125–128) it will then be shown how the relative *quantities* of employment, physical outputs and trade flows are determined in an international equilibrium. Finally, in the next chapter, it will be shown explicitly how consumption levels in the two countries have already been determined (implicitly) in the foregoing arguments, by the requirement that trade be balanced.

EQUILIBRIUM WITH GIVEN WAGE RATES

Suppose first, then, that the wage rate is exogenously determined in each country, being $\bar{w}^X$ in Xeres and $\bar{w}^Z$ in Zend. The given wage rates, together with the technical conditions of production in Xeres and Zend, will determine which of the Figs. 9.1 applies—it being understood, of course, that with given wage rates all the CM_1 and CM_2 lines of semi-specialisation in Fig. 9.1 will be curved. Since the nature of the argument is the same whichever figure applies, suppose for concreteness that it is Fig. 9.1(a).

It has already been established that the further along XYZ lie the prices (P_1, P_2), the higher will be r^X and the lower will be r^Z. The question now arises whether there exists a pair of prices (P_1, P_2), lying on XYZ, such that, at those prices,

$$s^X r^X = s^Z r^Z \tag{7}$$

where s^X and s^Z are the capitalists' savings ratios in Xeres and Zend respectively. For if there are prices for which (7) will hold, then they will be the equilibrium international prices, since they will be prices such that the freely chosen production and trading decisions adopted by the capitalists of Xeres and of Zend can be consistent with one another and with the maintenance of steady growth at the rate $g = s^X r^X = s^Z r^Z$.

Fig. 9.5 shows the xy and yz frontiers for r^X and r^Z; as was noted above, with given wage rates $\bar{w}^X$ and $\bar{w}^Z$, (5) defines a non-linear, inverse relation between r^X and r^Z, while (6) defines a linear, inverse relation between r^X and r^Z. Also shown in Fig. 9.5 is the graph of the relation $r^Z = (s^X/s^Z)r^X$, which is, of course, an upward sloping straight line passing through the origin. Now provided that, as will be assumed here, that line passes between x and z, it will necessarily intersect the frontier xyz at a unique point, labelled e in Fig. 9.5. The profit rates r_e^X and r_e^Z at point e will be the profit rates associated with an international equilibrium, in which the two economies grow

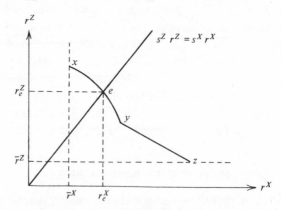

Fig. 9.5

at the common, steady rate given by $g_e = s^X r_e^X = s^Z r_e^Z$. The point e on xy in Fig. 9.5 will, of course, be associated with a particular point, call it E, lying on XY in Fig. 9.1(a), the prices (P_1^E, P_2^E) at that point being the equilibrium international prices. Since the equilibrium prices lie on XY in Fig. 9.1(a), it follows that the international equilibrium will involve the capitalists in Xeres choosing to produce C and M_1, the former being exported, while those in Zend choose to produce and export M_2 machines. (Of course, if the line $r^Z = (s^X/s^Z)r^X$ in Fig. 9.5 were to intersect yz rather than xy, then the equilibrium international prices would lie on YZ in Fig. 9.1(a) and thus the Xeres capitalists would produce and export C, while those in Zend would produce M_1 and M_2 machines, exporting the former.)

An international equilibrium has thus been shown to exist, under the assumptions made above, with the associated prices, profit rates, growth rate and patterns of production and trade all having been determined. As has already been noted, the technical conditions of production in Xeres and Zend together with the given wage rates $\bar{w}^X$ and $\bar{w}^Z$, suffice to determine which of the Figs. 9.1 applies and to determine the associated xyz frontier. As is apparent from Fig. 9.5, the xyz frontier and the two savings ratios, s^X and s^Z, determine the equilibrium profit rates and thus, implicitly, the equilibrium values of the other relevant variables. It may thus be said that the international equilibrium is determined by the technical conditions of production, the exogenously given wage rates and the two capitalists' savings ratios. (The physical *quantities* involved will be discussed below.)

Some comparative dynamics

Consider now an autarkic economy, $\bar{X}$, having the same production methods, wage rate and capitalists' savings ratio as the trading economy Xeres. The profit rate in $\bar{X}$ will, of course, be $\bar{r}^X < r_e^X$ and hence the growth rate in $\bar{X}$ will be $\bar{g}^X = s^X \bar{r}^X < s^X r_e^X = g_e$; the growth rate will be smaller in the autarkic economy, $\bar{X}$, than in the trading one, Xeres. Exactly the same argument may be repeated for a closed economy, $\bar{Z}$, which is otherwise similar to Zend. Hence the common, steady growth rate, g_e, applying to the trading economies Xeres and Zend, will be greater than the growth rate in either of the autarkic economies, $\bar{X}$ and $\bar{Z}$. Thus it may be said, rather loosely perhaps, that in the present framework the (positive) 'gain from trade' is that both trading economies can grow faster than they could do under autarkic conditions.

If any of the relevant technical coefficients had been higher — or either of the given wage rates lower — than was assumed in drawing Fig. 9.5 then, provided that Fig. 9.1(a) still applied, the frontier xyz in Fig. 9.5 would have been 'further out' from the origin. Hence with s^X and s^Z unchanged, r_e^X, r_e^Z and g_e would all have been greater; the equilibrium rates of profit and growth are thus positively related to productive efficiency but inversely related to wage rates.

Taking efficiency and wage rates to be fixed now, suppose that s^Z had been greater than was assumed in drawing Fig. 9.5; the line $r^Z = (s^X/s^Z)r^X$ would have been lower, hence r_e^X would have been greater and thus $g_e = s^X r_e^X$ would have been greater. If, on the other hand, s^X had been greater than assumed in Fig. 9.5, then r_e^Z would have been greater and thus, again, $g_e = s^Z r_e^Z$ would have been greater. Hence the common equilibrium growth rate is positively related to both savings ratios, while the equilibrium rate of profit in each country is inversely related to the savings ratio in that country but positively related to the savings ratio in the other country.

EQUILIBRIUM WITH ONE GROWTH RATE, ONE WAGE RATE GIVEN

Suppose now that the rate of growth is exogenously determined in one country, say at $\bar{g}^X$ in Xeres, while there is a given wage rate in the other ($\bar{w}^Z$ in Zend). Thus Xeres might, for example, be an advanced capitalist economy and Zend a backward one. An international equilibrium must now necessarily involve growth at the common rate $\bar{g}^X$, so that the equilibrium profit rate in Zend would have to be given by $r_e^Z = (\bar{g}^X/s^Z)$.

Whichever of Figs. 9.1 applies — with curved CM_1 and CM_2 lines for country Z — the further along XYZ are international prices (P_1, P_2), the lower will be r^Z. Thus an international equilibrium will exist if there are prices, on XYZ, such that $r^Z = r_e^Z$, where $s^Z r_e^Z = \bar{g}^X$. Provided that there are such prices, the existence of an international equilibrium will have been established and the corresponding values of $(P_1^E, P_2^E), r_e^Z, w_e^X$ and the patterns of production and trade will have been determined. The determinants of this equilibrium will be the technical conditions of production in Xeres and Zend, the given growth and wage rates, $\bar{g}^X$ and $\bar{w}^Z$, and the two savings ratios. (It should be noted that s^X plays a role in this determination by influencing $r_e^X = (\bar{g}^X/s^X)$ and thus affecting which of Figs. 9.1 applies.)

Introducing, as before, autarkic economies $\bar{X}$ and $\bar{Z}$, which are otherwise similar to the trading economies Xeres and Zend respectively, it can be shown—as the reader may check—that, if an international equilibrium exists, it will be such that $w_e^X > \bar{w}^X$ and $r_e^Z > \bar{r}^Z$, i.e. such that Xeres has a higher wage rate than $\bar{X}$, while Zend has higher profit and growth rates than has $\bar{Z}$. The (positive) 'gain from trade' might thus be said to take a different form in each country.

As long as the same Fig. 9.1 continues to apply, it will be clear that the equilibrium value of the profit rate in Zend, r_e^Z, is positively related to $\bar{g}^X$ but inversely related to s^Z, while the equilibrium value of the wage rate in Xeres, w_e^X, is related in precisely the opposite manner to $\bar{g}^X$ and s^Z. However, while r_e^Z will be quite independent of s^X, of $\bar{w}^Z$ and of the level of efficiency—being simply equal to $(\bar{g}^X/s^Z)$—w_e^X will depend on those factors, being positively related to the level of efficiency and to the savings ratio s^X but being inversely related to the level of $\bar{w}^Z$. (The last two relations follow from the facts that a higher level of s^X implies a lower level of r_e^X and that w_e^X is inversely related to all the other three wage and profit rates.)

EQUILIBRIUM WITH GIVEN GROWTH RATES

If the rate of growth is exogenously determined in each of the two countries, then there are two distinct cases to be considered, since the given growth rates may or may not be equal.

Equal given growth rates. Consider first the case in which each country has the same given rate of growth, say $\bar{g}$: it will be clear that such an equality constitutes a rather 'marginal' case and it is therefore not surprising that the implied international equilibrium is not fully determinate. The equilibrium rates of profit will, of course, be given by $s^X r_e^X = \bar{g}$ and $s^Z r_e^Z = \bar{g}$. These profit rates, together with the conditions of production in Xeres and Zend will determine which of Figs. 9.1 applies and will define an xyz frontier, giving an inverse relation between the wage rates w^X and w^Z, comparable to that shown in Fig. 9.4. To each (P_1, P_2) lying on XYZ in the appropriate Fig. 9.1, there will be a corresponding pair of wage rates (w^X, w^Z) lying on xyz but, by contrast with the cases considered above, there is, as yet, no method at hand to determine which (P_1, P_2) and which (w^X, w^Z) will be the equilibrium prices and wage rates. To render the system determinate it would be necessary to make some further assumption; for example, that trade union activity in either Xeres or Zend set the real wage rate in that country. The wage rate in the other country would then be determined through xyz (being lower, the higher the exogenously determined wage rate) and hence equilibrium prices and the patterns of production and trade would also be determined.

The w^X/w^Z frontier, xyz, would naturally be 'further out' from the origin the greater were the level of productivity and the two savings ratios, s^X and s^Z, and the lower were the common, given growth rate, $\bar{g}$.

Unequal given growth rates. Suppose now, by contrast with the assumption made elsewhere in this chapter, that the two countries have different given rates of growth satisfying, say, $\bar{g}^X > \bar{g}^Z$. It will be clear that, with Xeres becoming ever larger relative to Zend, there is no possibility of capitalists in Xeres permanently maintaining a specialisation or even a semi-specialisation, for the capitalists in Zend would eventually find it physically impossible to meet the import requirements of those in Xeres. The only sustainable situation in this case is, then, that all three commodities should be produced in Xeres; it follows immediately that autarky wages, profits and prices prevail in Xeres, so that $w_e^X = \bar{w}^X$, $r_e^X = \bar{r}^X$, $(P_1^E, P_2^E) = (p_1^X, p_2^X)$. International trade will have no effect on the wage rate and profit rate in Xeres and, far from trade influencing commodity prices in Xeres, the equilibrium international prices (P_1^E, P_2^E) will be completely determined by conditions in that country.

The equilibrium rate of profit in Zend will simply be given by $s^Z r_e^Z = \bar{g}^Z$; assuming that Zend capitalists adopt a complete specialisation at the *international* prices (p_1^X, p_2^X), the wage rate w_e^Z will be determined by the appropriate wage–profit–price equation for that specialisation and will naturally be greater than $\bar{w}^Z$, the wage for an autarkic economy $\bar{Z}$, otherwise similar to Zend.

While the wage rates, profit rates and prices discussed above will remain constant through time, the allocation of labour in the faster growing country, Xeres, will have to change through time. As can easily be shown, and as is intuitively obvious, as total employment in Zend relative to that in Xeres continually falls, the proportion of labour in Xeres which is devoted to producing the commodity also produced in Zend will have to increase steadily. As Zend becomes vanishingly small *relative* to Xeres, the allocation of labour in Xeres will, of course, tend toward the allocation for the closed economy, discussed in part I of chapter 3.

INTERNATIONAL ALLOCATION OF LABOUR

The brief remarks in the last paragraph aside, nothing has been said thus far about the relative *magnitudes* of employment levels, physical outputs and trade flows in an international equilibrium. Since the physical output and trade flows are directly and simply related to the employment levels, attention will be focussed here on the determination of the relative sizes of Xeres and Zend, as measured by their use of labour, together with that of the allocation of labour between the two industries of the semi-specialised country. The following results relating to the international allocation of labour may readily be translated into results concerning the relative magnitudes of output and trade flows.

It will be assumed throughout this section that Xeres and Zend have the same equilibrium growth rate, g. As is to be expected in a steady growth analysis, only *relative* employment levels will be considered, there being no question of determining absolute levels. It is to be noted that the labour quantities referred to are all quantities of labour *employed*; there is no presumption that there is full employment in either country. (Indeed, it is almost certain that there cannot be full employment in both countries, for only by a fluke will the ratio of labour use in Xeres and Zend be equal to the ratio of labour availabilities in the two countries.)

Consider the international prices lying on XYZ in Fig. 9.1. Leaving aside the singular points X, Y and Z themselves, it will be seen that such prices always induce one of the four possible patterns of production and trade shown in Table 9.1. (It will be left to the reader to analyse the production and trade patterns corresponding to equilibria at singular points.) In pattern 1, for example, induced by prices lying on YZ in Fig. 9.1(a), C is produced in Xeres while M_1 and M_2 are produced in Zend, C being exported from Xeres and M_1 machines being exported from Zend. Pattern 3, it will be noted, is the only one in which all three commodities are traded, so that, as was noted above, a *tradeable* commodity may well

Table 9.1

Pattern	Prices lie on	Positive outputs			Exports		
1	YZ in Fig. 9.1(a)	C^X	M_1^Z	M_2^Z	C^X	M_1^Z	
2	XY in Figs. 9.1(a), (b)	C^X	M_1^X	M_2^Z	C^X	M_2^Z	
3	YZ in Figs. 9.1(b), (c)	C^Z	M_1^X	M_2^Z	C^Z	M_1^X	M_2^Z
4	XY in Fig. 9.1(c)	C^Z	M_1^X	M_2^X	C^Z	M_1^X	

not be a *traded* commodity. (It should perhaps be remarked that exports of C or M_2 will never absorb the total output of those commodities—some of the output being required for domestic consumption or for further M_2 production—but that exports of M_1 machines will absorb the whole of M_1 production, for M_1 machines will be exported only if C production takes place in the other country and in such a case there is no domestic use for M_1 machines.)

Suppose then that equilibrium international prices lie on YZ in Fig. 9.1(a), so that pattern 1 obtains; let total labour use in Xeres be L^X and that in Zend be L^Z, the latter being divided between L_1^Z and L_2^Z in M_1 and M_2 production respectively. The output of M_1 machines, $m_1^Z L_1^Z$, must equal the requirement for those machines in Xeres, which is $(1+g)L^X$; the output of M_2 machines, $m_2^Z L_2^Z$, must provide for the replacement and expansion requirements of both the M_1 and M_2 industries, which total $(1+g)L^Z$. Hence:

$$m_1^Z L_1^Z = (1+g)L^X \tag{8}$$
$$m_2^Z L_2^Z = (1+g)L^Z \tag{9}$$

It follows from (8) and (9) that

$$(L_1^Z/L_2^Z) = \left[\left(\frac{m_2^Z}{1+g}\right) - 1\right] \tag{10}$$

$$(L^X/L^Z) = \left(\frac{m_1^Z}{m_2^Z}\right)\left[\left(\frac{m_2^Z}{1+g}\right) - 1\right] \tag{11}$$

Result (10) shows the proportional allocation of labour within Zend as a function of the growth rate g, while (11) shows how the relative sizes of Xeres and Zend, as measured by labour use, depend on g. (It will be seen, from (11), that the relative size of the country in which M_2 machines are produced, Zend, will be higher the higher is the growth rate.) When an international equilibrium involves outputs and exports in pattern 1, the international allocation of labour will be determined by (10) and (11), since m_1^Z, m_2^Z and g will all be known.

It may be seen from Table 9.1 that the outputs and exports in pattern 4 can be obtained from those of pattern 1 by simply interchanging the superscripts X and Z. It follows immediately that, with X and Z interchanged, results (10) and (11) determine the international allocation of labour in an international equilibrium involving outputs and exports in pattern 4.

Consider now pattern 2 in Table 9.1. Using an obvious notation, the following relations must obtain:

$$L_C^X + L_1^X = L^X$$
$$m_1^X L_1^X = (1 + g)L_C^X$$
$$m_2^Z L^Z = (1 + g)(L_1^X + L^Z)$$

If follows that:

$$(L_C^X/L_1^X) = [m_1^X/(1 + g)] \tag{12}$$

$$(L^X/L^Z) = \left[\left(\frac{m_2^Z}{1 + g}\right) - 1\right]\left[\left(\frac{m_1^X}{1 + g}\right) + 1\right] \tag{13}$$

Relations (12) and (13) determine the international allocation of labour in a pattern 2 international equilibrium. (As in patterns 1 and 4, the relative size of the country in which M_2 machines are produced will be greater the greater is the equilibrium growth rate.)

Pattern 3, the one pattern in which all three commodities are traded, remains to be considered. In an obvious notation, the following must hold:

$$L_C^Z + L_2^Z = L^Z$$
$$m_1^X L^X = (1 + g)L_C^Z$$
$$m_2^Z L_2^Z = (1 + g)(L^X + L_2^Z)$$

It follows that:

$$(L_C^Z/L_2^Z) = \left\{\frac{m_1^X[m_2^Z - (1 + g)]}{(1 + g)^2}\right\} \tag{14}$$

$$(L^X/L^Z) = \left\{\frac{[m_2^Z - (1 + g)](1 + g)}{m_1^X[m_2^Z - (1 + g)] + (1 + g)^2}\right\} \tag{15}$$

Relations (14) and (15) determine the international allocation of labour in a pattern 3 international equilibrium. (By contrast with patterns 1, 2 and 4, it is not possible here to say that the greater is the growth rate, the greater will be the relative size of the country, Zend, in which M_2 machines are produced. (L^X/L^Z) falls monotonically as g rises from zero if and only if $m_2^Z \geq m_1^X(m_2^Z - 1)^2$; otherwise it rises at first and then falls. Since Xeres is specialised in the production of M_1 machines, this result is precisely analogous to the finding, in chapter 3, that in a closed economy the proportion of total labour use which is accounted for by the M_1 industry can be either positively or negatively related to the rate of growth.)

It may be concluded that, no matter which XY or YZ line in Fig. 9.1 the equilibrium international prices may lie upon (provided that they do not fall at a singular point X, Y or Z), the relevant conditions of production and the equilibrium rate of growth will suffice to determine the equilibrium allocation of labour use, both as between the countries and as between the two industries of the semi-specialised country. (If international prices should lie exactly at Y in Fig. 9.1 then, of course, the international allocation of labour will not be fully determined and the ratio L^X/L^Z will merely be constrained to lie between the ratios which apply when prices lie strictly on the relevant XY or YZ lines.)

SUMMARY

A very simple analysis of international equilibrium has been presented, in the context of a two country, three commodity world in which all three commodities are tradeable, there is no choice of technique and both countries exhibit steady growth (for the most part, at a common rate of growth). It was seen that, for any pattern of international specialisation, an 'international wage–profit frontier' may be derived, showing how the real wage rates and the profit rates in the two countries are related to one another; for given values of any two of those four distributive variables, the remaining two distributive variables are inversely related. It was also noted that to any point on an international wage–profit frontier there corresponds a particular set of international relative prices. The international wage–profit frontier was then used to examine the existence and comparative dynamic properties of international equilibrium for different combinations of exogenously given real wage rate(s) and/or growth rate(s) in the two countries.

The proximate determinants of international equilibrium were found, in each case, to be (i) the properties of the available methods of production in each economy (ii) the capitalists' savings ratios in each economy and (iii) the levels of the exogenously given real wage and/or growth rates. The traditional concept of 'comparative advantage' was employed but was found to be most relevant in relation to the production of the machines, M_1 and M_2, and to bear more fully on the location of their production than on the pattern of trade. It was noted that, while all three commodities were assumed to be *tradeable*, all three would in fact be *traded* in only one of the four possible patterns of international specialisation—that in which the fully specialised country produces the 'intermediate' M_1 machines. It was also remarked that it is not necessarily true that all international equilibrium price ratios lie between the two corresponding autarky price ratios.

The above results refer to prices, real wage rates and rates of profit and growth; it was also seen how, in equilibrium, the relative employment levels in the two countries, and the allocation of labour in the non-specialised country, are determined in terms of conditions of production and the equilibrium growth rate. It was noted that the relative size (in terms of employment) of the country producing the 'basic' machine, M_2, is an increasing function of the equilibrium growth rate (unless the fully specialised country produces the 'intermediate' machine, M_1, in which case such a positive relation is ensured only for 'sufficiently' high growth rates).

No explicit reference has been made in this chapter to consumption levels or the 'gain from trade'. These matters are taken up in the next chapter, which also presents a slightly more sophisticated version of the above analysis and shows how it can be generalised to deal with trade policy, non-tradeables, many commodities, many countries and a choice of technique in each country.

10

INTERNATIONAL EQUILIBRIUM
FURTHER CONSIDERED

The analysis of international equilibrium which was presented in chapter 9 was carried out under very simple assumptions and made no explicit reference to consumption levels or to the balance of trade. In this chapter, therefore, it will be shown how consumption levels and the growth rate are related in international equilibrium and how the consumption optimality or non-optimality of trade may be analysed in that context. It will then be shown how an international equilibrium with constant rates of unemployment might be determined. Attention will also be drawn to the possibility of allowing for tariffs, etc., and for the presence of non-tradeable commodities, in the analysis of international equilibrium. Finally, it will be considered how the analysis may be extended to the case of many countries, many commodities and many alternative production methods. In the interest of simplicity, it will be assumed throughout that, in international equilibrium, both (or all) countries grow at a common, steady growth rate.

CONSUMPTION AND GROWTH

To show the relations which must obtain between levels of consumption per unit of employment and the rate of growth, one need only render explicit what has already been demonstrated, albeit implicitly, in chapter 9. Whichever pattern of production and international allocation of labour might be involved in an international equilibrium, total consumption must be equal to the quantity of C produced, so that, in an obvious notation,

$$c^X L^X + c^Z L^Z = q^i L_C^i \qquad (1)$$

where $i = X$ or Z according as C is produced in Xeres or Zend. (If C is produced in a completely specialised country then $L_C^i = L^i$, of course.) Now it was shown in chapter 9 that, for each non-singular pattern of production and trade, the international allocation of labour is determined as a known function of the growth rate, g. Hence by substituting the appropriate functions of g for the ratios between the labour quantities in (1), one can obtain a relationship between c^X, c^Z and g.

Thus suppose that, in an international equilibrium, prices lie on YZ of Fig. 9.1(a), so that outputs fall into pattern 1 of Table 9.1; capitalists in Xeres adopt a C specialisation, so $L_C^X = L^X$. Then on setting $i = X$ and dividing through by L^X in (1) above and making use of (11) from chapter 9, one obtains the 'international consumption–growth frontier':

$$c^X + \left\{ \frac{m_2^Z(1+g)}{m_1^Z[m_2^Z - (1+g)]} \right\} c^Z = q^X \qquad (2)$$

It will be seen from (2) that, for any given value of g, the consumption levels c^X and c^Z are inversely related, that c^Z and g are inversely related for any given level of c^X and that c^X and g are inversely related for any given (positive) level of c^Z.

The finding that any two of c^X, c^Z and g are inversely related is clearly analogous to the result that, in a closed economy, c and g are so related (see chapter 3). Since the consumption–growth frontier is identical to the wage–profit frontier in a closed economy, it is natural to ask whether a similar correspondence exists in the international context. The international wage–profit frontier for a pattern 1 international equilibrium is given by equation (6) of chapter 9; on setting $w^X = c^X$, $w^Z = c^Z$ and $r^X = r^Z = g$ in that equation, one finds that it becomes equation (2) above. The international consumption–growth frontier is identical to the international wage–profit frontier, when the latter is restricted to the case of equal profit rates in the two countries.

The international consumption–growth frontiers for the other three patterns of production and trade are just as easily found. That for pattern 4 is, of course, simply (2) above with X and Z interchanged. The frontier for a pattern 2 equilibrium can be shown, from (1) above and (12) and (13) of chapter 9, to be

$$(m_1^X + 1 + g)c^X + \left[\frac{(1+g)^2}{m_2^Z - (1+g)} \right] c^Z = m_1^X q^X \qquad (3)$$

(Relation (3) may also be derived by setting $w^X = c^X$, $w^Z = c^Z$ and $r^X = r^Z = g$ in the wage–profit frontier (5) of chapter 9.) The frontier for a pattern 3 equilibrium, found from (1) above and (14) and (15) of chapter 9, is

$$(1+g)c^X + \left\{ m_1^X + \left[\frac{(1+g)^2}{m_2^Z - (1+g)} \right] \right\} c^Z = m_1^X q^Z \qquad (4)$$

It will be seen from (3) and (4) that for any given value of c^X or c^Z or g, the other two variables are inversely related, just as in (2), since in each case the coefficients of both c^X and c^Z are increasing functions of g. (Relation (4) can also be derived directly, of course, from the corresponding wage–profit frontier.)

The above analysis does not, by itself, suffice to determine the values of c^X and c^Z in an international equilibrium. In such an equilibrium, it is known which pattern of production and trade will apply and hence which of the above international consumption–growth frontiers has to be considered. It is also known what the equilibrium growth rate, g_e, will be and thus, on setting $g = g_e$ in the appropriate equation—(2), (3) or (4)—above, it will be found that c^X and c^Z must satisfy a known linear equation. To determine the equilibrium values of c^X and c^Z, it is now sufficient to assume that trade is balanced, to note that one of the two countries is always completely specialised (in a non-singular equilibrium) and to recall from chapter 5 that the consumption level in a completely specialised economy is always determined in terms of international prices and the growth rate. Since, in an international equilibrium, the prices and the growth rate are determined and it is known which country is completely specialised and in which commodity, it follows that the level of consumption per unit of employment in that country is already determined. The consumption level in the other country then follows immediately from the known linear equation, linking c^X and c^Z, which was mentioned above. Hence implicit in the determination of an international equilibrium, discussed in chapter 9, was the determination of the associated equilibrium consumption levels, c_e^X and c_e^Z. The equilibrium consumption levels per unit of employment are thus determined by the available methods of production, by the savings ratios s^X and s^Z and by the exogenously given wage and/or growth rates.

THE CONSUMPTION-OPTIMALITY OF TRADE AND THE GAIN FROM TRADE

It was seen in chapter 3 that, in a closed economy, a capitalist, profit-maximising choice of technique may or may not be optimal in terms of the level of consumption compatible with a given growth rate, except, of course, in the case of the rates of profit and growth being equal. In chapter 5, it was then found that the specialisation adopted by capitalists in a trading economy might or might not be consumption-optimal (subject again to the condition $g < r$), since a choice of specialisation is, in effect, a choice of technique. It is not to be expected, then, that an international equilibrium will necessarily be consumption-optimal for both countries (unless $s^X = s^Z = 1$, so that $r_e^X = r_e^Z = g_e$). To avoid the ambiguity which can arise concerning the gain from trade when the wage is exogenously determined, attention will be confined here to the rather restrictive case of equal, exogenously given growth rates in the two countries ($\bar{g}^X = \bar{g}^Z = \bar{g} = g_e$).

Consider Figs. 5.2, each of which shows, not only the lines of semi-specialisation corresponding to a given rate of profit, $\bar{r}$, but also the division of the set of non-negative (P_1, P_2) into regions giving the specialisation which is consumption-optimal for a given growth rate, $\bar{g}$. Leaving aside the marginal possibility that (P_1, P_2) might lie at the intersection of a solid and a broken line, it will be seen that a CM_1 or a CM_2 semi-specialisation is necessarily non-optimal for consumption. On the other hand, an M_1M_2 semi-specialisation is necessarily consumption-optimal when $m_1 \geq m_2$, while it may or may not be optimal when $m_1 < m_2$. Since a non-singular international equilibrium necessarily involves that the capitalists of one country adopt a semi-specialisation, these observations alone provide some information about the consumption-optimality of an international equilibrium. If that equilibrium involves a CM_1 or a CM_2 semi-specialisation, as it does on XY in Figs. 9.1(a), (b) and on YZ in Figs. 9.1(b), (c), it may be said immediately that the equilibrium is non-optimal for consumption in at least one of the countries. On the other hand, if equilibrium prices lie on YZ in Fig. 9.1(a) or XY in Fig. 9.1(c), then one country is semi-specialised in M_1 and M_2 production so that, if $m_1 \geq m_2$ for that country, the equilibrium is consumption-optimal for at least one country.

Suppose now that $m_1^X < m_2^X$ and $m_1^Z < m_2^Z$, so that Fig. 5.2(c) applies to both Xeres and Zend, given that s^X, s^Z are less than unity. If the conditions of production and the given profit rates $\bar{r}^X$ and $\bar{r}^Z$ are such that the relative positions of the Xeres and Zend lines of semi-specialisation are as shown in Fig. 9.1(b), then Fig. 10.1 below will apply. Fig. 10.1 shows the semi-specialisation lines for both Xeres and Zend and the lines separating optimal and non-optimal consumption regions for Zend; the consumption lines for Xeres are omitted in the interest of clarity. If the international equilibrium prices should lie at E_1 in Fig. 10.1, then the equilibrium will be non-optimal for Xeres but optimal for Zend, while if they should lie at E_2 the equilibrium will be non-optimal for both countries. A very similar

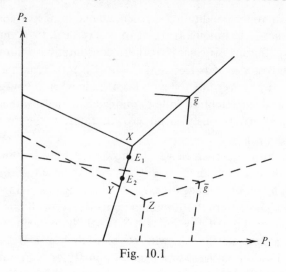

Fig. 10.1

argument can be used to show that if, for example, international equilibrium prices lie on XY in Fig. 9.1(c) and $m_1^X > m_2^X$, $m_1^Z > m_2^Z$, then that equilibrium can be consumption-optimal for both Xeres and Zend.

It may thus be concluded that an international equilibrium may be consumption-optimal for both countries, optimal for one but not for the other, or non-optimal for both.

An equilibrium which is consumption-optimal for both countries will naturally yield a positive 'gain from trade' to both countries, each of which will have a higher consumption level than, and the same growth rate as, an otherwise similar autarkic economy. It was seen in chapter 5, however, that, for a single economy, non-optimal consumption may or may not involve a 'loss from trade'; similar arguments apply in the present context. (For example, if an equilibrium is non-optimal for both countries, then both may still gain, one gain and the other lose, or both lose from trade.) A full investigation of this issue, best carried out by means of the alternative technique of analysis introduced at the end of chapter 4, would, however, prove rather unrewarding and the matter will not be pursued here.

EQUILIBRIUM WITH CONSTANT RATES OF UNEMPLOYMENT

In the discussion of different kinds of international equilibrium presented in chapter 9, no reference was made to the rate of growth of the labour supply in either country. Yet it is clear that steady growth, at a rate g, can persist for a long period only if it is true, for each country, either that the country starts the period with a sufficiently large reserve of unemployed labour or that the supply of labour grows at a rate greater than or equal to g. While the analysis of growth paths with either decreasing or increasing percentage rates of unemployment is certainly of significance, it may also be of interest to ask whether international equilibria can obtain in which the common rate of growth of the two countries is equal, in each country, to the rate of growth of the labour supply, so that the percentage rate of unemployment in each country is constant.

The growth rate of the labour supply

It is self-evident that, flukes aside, no international equilibrium with equal labour force growth rates can exist, unless at least one of those growth rates is dependent on one or more endogenous variables. The simplest assumption to make is that, in each country, the rate of growth of the labour supply is an increasing function of that country's real wage rate, at least for sufficiently low values of that wage rate. This simple assumption also has some plausibility, both because there is, presumably, a real wage level so low that the working class would cease to reproduce itself and because the effective supply of labour may well be more responsive to the real wage level than is the mere number of potential workers. (Thus the rates of change of the average length of life of a worker, the number of hours worked, the strength and efficiency of the worker, and the overall participation rate may all depend on the level of real wages.) On the other hand, the growth rate of the effective labour supply might become independent of the real wage rate at sufficiently high levels of the latter.

It will be clear that in postulating the existence of a stable relationship between the rate of growth of effective labour supply in a country and the real wage rate in that country, one is implicitly assuming both the absence of international labour migration and the maintenance of a reasonably stable social structure within the country in question. If either implicit assumption be dropped, the rate of growth of the effective labour supply in a country will come to depend on, e.g., real wage rates in other countries, changing legal controls on migration, changes in the rate at which peasants are being dispossessed of their land, and so on.

Consider then Fig. 10.2, the right-hand side of which shows how n^x, the rate of growth of the effective labour supply in Xeres, depends on w^x, the

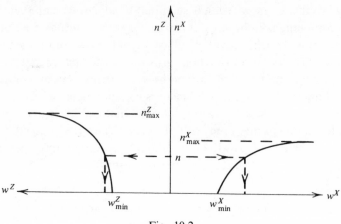

Fig. 10.2

real wage rate in Xeres. It is assumed that n^X is positive only for $w^X > w^X_{min}$ and that, as w^X increases, n^X eventually becomes constant at n^X_{max} The left-hand side of Fig. 10.2 exhibits a similar relationship for Zend, with $n^Z_{max} > n^X_{max}$. (The reader may subsequently vary either or both sides of Fig. 10.2 to examine other possible cases.)

By construction, when the wage rate in Xeres in w^X_{min} and that in Zend is w^Z_{min}, Xeres and Zend have equal (zero) growth rates of effective labour supply. The wage rates w^X and w^Z may now be notionally increased, in such a way that n^X and n^Z, though now positive, continue to be equal, with $n^X = n^Z = n$. Eventually, however, the point will be reached at which $n = n^X = n^Z = n^X_{max}$ so that there is only a finite range of values of w^X and w^Z for which $n^X = n^Z$. The curve UV in Fig. 10.3 shows those pairs of w^X and w^Z which imply equal growth rates of the effective labour supply in Xeres and Zend, the common growth rate, n, being zero at point U and increasing monotonically to n^X_{max} at point V.

Equilibrium

It was seen in chapter 9 that, for given, positive values of the capitalists' savings ratios in Xeres and Zend, s^X and s^Z, the trade equilibrium growth rate, g, is inversely related to each of the real wage rates, w^X and w^Z. It will be assumed that the growth rate g which corresponds to the wage levels $w^X = w^X_{min}$ and $w^Z = w^Z_{min}$ is either zero or positive; if it were negative then

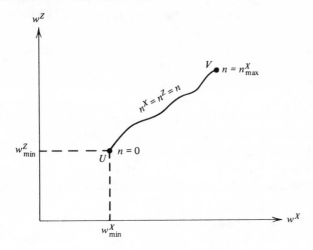

Fig. 10.3

no 'constant rates of unemployment equilibrium' could exist. If it should be zero, then such an equilibrium clearly would exist, with real wages at their 'minimum' levels, w^X_{min} and w^Z_{min}, in Xeres and Zend and with output, employment and effective labour supply being constant over time in each country.

Suppose, then, that with $w^X = w^X_{min}$ and $w^Z = w^Z_{min}$, trade equilibrium would involve a positive growth rate of output. We may now notionally increase w^X and w^Z along UV in Fig. 10.3; the common rate of growth of effective labour supply in Xeres and Zend, n, will increase from zero, while the growth rate of output in a trade equilibrium, g, will decrease. There are two possibilities: either $g = n$ at some pair of wage rates lying on UV or even at point $V, g > n = n^X_{max}$. In the first case, the existence of an international equilibrium with constant rates of unemployment has been established, for the given values of the savings ratios s^X, s^Z.

In the second case, however, it has been shown that no such equilibrium exists, with the given savings ratios. Suppose, then, that these savings ratios are now considered to be variables, rather than given data. Holding w^X and w^Z constant at the levels corresponding to point V in Fig. 10.3, we may notionally decrease s^X and s^Z, maintaining their ratio constant. Now it was shown in chapter 9 that, with given real wage rates, the growth rate of output in a trade equilibrium is an increasing function of each savings ratio. Thus as s^X and s^Z are decreased, the trade equilibrium growth rate,

g, will decrease and will, indeed, fall towards zero as s^X and s^Z approach zero. It follows that it will be possible to lower s^X and s^Z until $g = n^X_{max}$ and thus a constant rate of unemployment equilibrium is obtained. If s^X and s^Z are lowered still further, such an equilibrium can be maintained, of course, by an appropriate decrease of w^X, w^Z along UV, towards U.

It may thus be concluded that if, in both Xeres and Zend, the relation between the growth rate of the effective labour supply and the real wage rate is as shown in Fig. 10.2, then an international equilibrium, with a constant rate of unemployment in each country, will always exist for sufficiently low savings ratios s^X and s^Z. For arbitrarily given values of s^X and s^Z, however, such an equilibrium may or may not exist: if it does exist, it is unique.

The foregoing statements, it should be noted explicitly, refer only to the *existence* of combinations of w^X, w^Z, s^X and s^Z for which an equilibrium of the kind considered will exist. No statement has been made as to whether —or how—such a combination could be achieved. If there are forces preventing the achievement of such a combination, as there might well be, then it is simply to be concluded that such an equilibrium will not obtain.

Comparison of international equilibrium with autarkic equilibria

Assuming now that an international equilibrium, with constant rates of unemployment, exists for the exogenously given savings ratios, that equilibrium may be compared with the corresponding autarkic equilibria in Xeres and Zend. Let $\bar{w}^X$ and $\bar{w}^Z$ be the real wage rates yielding *autarkic* equilibrium, with a constant rate of unemployment, in Xeres and Zend respectively. Without loss of generality, suppose that the autarky growth rates are such that $\bar{n}^X > \bar{n}^Z$. Holding w^X constant at $\bar{w}^X$, notionally increase w^Z to $\hat{w}^Z$ at which $n^Z = \bar{n}^X$; by construction, the wage rates $\bar{w}^X$ and $\hat{w}^Z$ lie on UV in Fig. 10.3.

Now, holding w^X and w^Z constant at $\bar{w}^X$, $\hat{w}^Z$ respectively, we know that trade equilibrium would involve a growth rate, g, greater than $n^X = n^Z = \bar{n}^X$. Thus by notionally increasing w^X and w^Z—from $\bar{w}^X$, $\hat{w}^Z$—along UV in Fig. 10.3, the common labour supply growth rate will increase and g will decrease. By assumption, there is a point on UV at which an international 'constant rates of unemployment' equilibrium obtains. It has now been shown that, in such an equilibrium, the real wage rate will exceed the corresponding autarky wage rate in each country, while the growth rate will exceed each autarky growth rate.

TARIFFS AND INTERNATIONAL EQUILIBRIUM

It was seen in chapters 6 and 7 how tariffs, subsidies, multiple exchange rates, etc., could influence the pattern of specialisation, and domestic prices and income distribution, in a small economy facing given international prices. It must now be considered what effects such trade policies will have in the context of an international equilibrium, for there is no presumption that the equilibrium international prices will be independent of the levels of tariffs, etc. Since it was shown in chapter 7 that the effects of non-tariff policies are in many respects similar to those of tariff policies, it will suffice here to consider tariff policy and, indeed, the discussion will be further restricted to the analysis of one particular kind of tariff. Once the method of approaching such questions has been firmly grasped, the reader should have no difficulty in extending the analysis to cover any kind of trade policy. The analysis will be confined to the case of exogenously given wage rates, $\bar{w}^X$ and $\bar{w}^Z$; the analysis would be little altered if an alternative closure of the system were assumed.

Suppose that, under free trade conditions, Fig. 9.1(a) would apply (with curved CM_1 and CM_2 lines of semi-specialisation), equilibrium international prices being on YZ. In a free trade equilibrium, then, the capitalists in Xeres would adopt a C specialisation. Consider now the effect of the imposition of an *ad valorem* tariff, at rate t_1^X, on any imports of M_1 machines into Xeres. The matter is best approached by showing how such a tariff will affect the international wage–profit frontiers.

It will be clear that a tariff t_1^X will have no effect at all on the international wage–profit frontier which would be involved if capitalists in Xeres adopted a CM_1 semi-specialisation, while those in Zend adopted an M_2 specialisation, for the simple reason that no M_1 machines would then be imported into Xeres. In this case, then, the frontier given by (5) of chapter 9 will continue to apply with, in the present context, $w^X = \bar{w}^X$ and $w^Z = \bar{w}^Z$. As was pointed out in chapter 9, with given wage rates $(\bar{w}^X, \bar{w}^Z)$ equation (5) of chapter 9 defines a non-linear inverse relation between r^X and r^Z, which is shown as xy'' in Fig. 10.4.

On the other hand, the presence of a positive tariff t_1^X will affect the international wage–profit frontier which applies when capitalists in Xeres adopt a C specialisation, while those in Zend adopt an M_1M_2 semi-specialisation; since a tariff is now levied on the imports of M_1 machines into Xeres, it is intuitively obvious that the r^X, r^Z frontier must be lower than the corresponding free trade frontier. Indeed it is easy to show that,

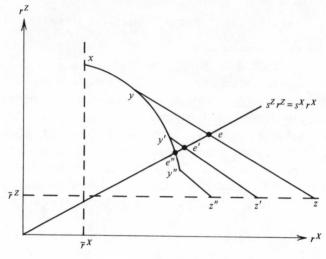

Fig. 10.4

in the present context, equation (6) of chapter 9 has to be replaced by:

$$(1 + t_1^X)m_2^Z\bar{w}^Z(1 + r^X) + m_1^Z(q^X - \bar{w}^X)(1 + r^Z) = m_1^Z m_2^Z(q^X - \bar{w}^X) \qquad (5)$$

It will be seen that (5) defines a linear, inverse relation between r^X and r^Z, which is 'further in' towards the origin the higher is the tariff rate t_1^X. In Fig. 10.4, yz shows the relevant part of the r^X, r^Z line, defined by (5), for the free trade case ($t_1^X = 0$); $y'z'$ shows the corresponding line for a certain positive tariff rate and $y''z''$ the line for a yet higher tariff rate.

As is shown in Fig. 10.4, under free trade conditions the equilibrium point, e, lies on yz, so that equilibrium prices lie on YZ in Fig. 9.1(a), as assumed at the outset of the present discussion. With a 'small' tariff rate, yielding the frontier $y'z'$ in Fig. 10.4, the equilibrium, at e', still involves a pattern 1 type equilibrium. The levying of the tariff t_1^X has not caused the pattern of production and trade to differ from the free trade pattern; it has, however, caused the equilibrium rates of profit and growth to be smaller than the free trade equilibrium rates. (Thus it might be said, somewhat loosely, that the government in Xeres has gained tariff revenue at the 'cost' of lowering the rate of growth in *both* countries.) Since the equilibrium value of r^Z is lower at e' than at e, it is not difficult to show, by considering the wage–profit–price equations for the production of machines, that the equilibrium values of both P_1 and P_2 are lower at e' than at e; the consumption commodity C, that is, is more expensive, relative to machines, in the with-tariff equilibrium than in the free trade equilibrium.

Consider now the effect of a 'large' tariff, t_1^X, yielding the frontier $y''z''$ in Fig. 10.4. The equilibrium point, e'', now lies on the xy'' frontier, not on the $y''z''$ frontier, implying that with a 'large' tariff the international equilibrium will be of the pattern 2 kind, with Xeres capitalists producing both C and M_1, while the Zend capitalists specialise in producing M_2 machines. Thus the levying of a 'large' potential tariff on M_1 imports into Xeres, has caused the equilibrium pattern of production and trade to differ from the free trade equilibrium pattern. In a purely comparative sense, it could be said that the tariff has 'shifted' M_1 production from Zend to Xeres and that the M_1 industry exists in Xeres only because it is protected by the tariff which would be levied on any M_1 imports. Hence the equilibrium pattern of production and trade depends, in general, on tariff policy; this being so in the present context just as it was in the case of a single, small economy facing given world prices.

It will be clear, from Fig. 10.4, that the equilibrium rates of profit and growth at e'' are lower than those at e and are, indeed, lower than those at e', even though, by contrast with the situation at e', no tariff revenue is generated at e''. By considering the various wage–profit–price relations which must hold, with either equality or inequality, at each of the equilibrium positions—e, e' and e'' in Fig. 10.4—it is not difficult to show that, in an obvious notation,

$$P_1^{E''} < P_1^{E'} < P_1^E$$
$$P_2^{E''} < P_2^{E'} < P_2^E$$

The equilibrium value of C, relative to the machines M_1 and M_2, is higher at e' than at e and higher still at e''.

The above analysis can easily be extended to allow for the possibility that a tariff, at rate t_C^Z, is levied on imports of corn into Zend. As the reader may check, when equations (5) and (6) of chapter 9 are modified to allow for the presence of the tariff at rate t_C^Z, it is found that both the xy frontier and the yz frontier will be lower the greater is t_C^Z. It follows that there are tariff structures, with positive t_1^X and t_C^Z, such that the xyz frontier in Fig. 10.4 will pass below the point $(\bar{r}^X, \bar{r}^Z)$, the implication being that specialisation and trade will not occur, both economies being autarkic.

The above example will suffice to show that, in the international equilibrium context, tariffs may or may not be prohibitive of trade and that, when not prohibitive, they may or may not cause the pattern of production and trade to differ from the free trade equilibrium pattern. With-tariff equilibrium prices will, however, differ from the free trade ones and the with-tariff equilibrium values of those wage rates and rates of profit and growth which are not exogenously determined will be lower than the corresponding free trade values. It will be seen that these conclusions are similar to those reached, in chapter 6, concerning the effects of tariffs in a single, small economy; the major differences are that, in the present context, tariffs can cause international prices to be different from what they would otherwise have been and that, as a result, tariffs imposed in one country can have significant effects on another country, in terms of prices, output patterns and income distribution.

Further on trade policy

It was seen earlier in this chapter that the free trade equilibrium pattern of production and trade could be consumption-optimal for both, one or neither of the two countries; it has now been found that tariffs might or might not cause the equilibrium pattern of production and trade to differ from the free trade equilibrium pattern. Hence, just as in the case of a single, small economy, one can have no *a priori* expectation concerning the effect of tariffs on the consumption optimality or non-optimality of trade. It follows that, in each country, the 'gain from trade' might be greater or smaller with tariffs than with free trade.

It would be a lengthy and not very rewarding process to show how each non-tariff trade policy can be analysed in an international equilibrium context; one example, of multiple exchange rate policy, must suffice. Consider together Fig. 7.2 and Fig. 9.1 and suppose that under free trade conditions Fig. 9.1(a) would apply. Now assume that the government in Zend applies a multiple exchange rate system, in which more units of domestic currency are exchanged for each unit of foreign currency when C exports or imports are involved than when M_1 or M_2 exports or imports are involved, the rate being the same for M_1 and M_2 transactions. Thus, in the notation of Fig. 7.2, $e_C > e_1 = e_2$. It will be seen from Fig. 7.2, that as e_C is (notionally) increased relative to e_1 and e_2, the M_1M_2 line of semi-specialisation will be unchanged but the CM_1 and CM_2 lines will move 'further out' from the origin; each will, in fact, move out without changing its slope. It follows that if Fig. 9.1(a) applies under free trade conditions $(e_C = e_1 = e_2)$ then, as e_C is made higher and higher relative to e_1 and e_2, first Fig. 9.1(b) will come to apply and then, at sufficiently high values of

e_C, Fig. 9.1(c) will come to apply. Since there is no pattern of production and trade common to Figs. 9.1(a) and (c), it follows immediately that multiple exchange rates can generate an international equilibrium involving a pattern of production and trade different from the free trade equilibrium pattern. In Fig. 9.1(a) no international equilibrium can involve the production of C in Zend: in Fig. 9.1(c), however, any international equilibrium will necessarily involve such production. In an equilibrium in Fig. 9.1(c), therefore, it may be said that the C industry exists in Zend because it is 'protected' by the multiple exchange rate policy which, with $e_C > e_1 = e_2$, clearly favours domestic production of C in Zend.

The reader may now examine in detail, making use of the international wage–profit frontiers which obtain when the government in Zend operates a multiple exchange rate system, how the equilibrium values of international prices and the endogenously determined wage rates and/or rates of profit and growth will depend upon the relative values of e_C, e_1 and e_2 in Zend.

NON-TRADEABLE COMMODITIES

It was seen in chapter 8 that, in the context of the simple C, M_1, M_2 model of production with no choice of technique, non-tradeable commodities were easily allowed for in the analysis of a single, small economy subject to free trade. It must now be shown that, by a simple extension of the results previously obtained, non-tradeable commodities can be allowed for in the analysis of international equilibrium. It will be assumed, as before, that there are just the three commodities, that there is no choice of technique in either country and that trade is free: it will also be assumed throughout that the C commodity has to be produced in at least one of the two countries and that the 'machine comparative advantage' condition, $(m_1^X/m_2^X) > (m_1^Z/m_2^Z)$, continues to hold.

M_2 non-tradeable

It was shown in chapter 8 that, with M_2 machines being non-tradeable, capitalists would adopt a C specialisation if $P_1 < p_1$ but would produce both M_2 and M_1 machines, exporting the latter and importing C, if $P_1 > p_1$. It follows immediately that if P_1 is to be an equilibrium international price, in a world consisting of the two countries Xeres and Zend, then P_1 must lie between p_1^X and p_1^Z. If $p_1^X > P_1 > p_1^Z$, then the positive outputs in international equilibrium will be C^X, M_1^Z and M_2^Z, with C being exported from Xeres and M_1 machines being exported from Zend; this is precisely a pattern 1 situation (see Table 9.1). If, on the other hand, $p_1^X < P_1 < p_1^Z$, then the position is simply reversed and a pattern 4 situation is obtained.

Suppose, then, that $p_1^X > p_1^Z$ so that an international equilibrium must involve a pattern 1 of production and trade. The wage–profit–price equations will simply be the equations which apply for the pattern 1 case when all commodities are tradeable, *except that* the international price of M_2 machines, P_2, will have to be replaced by the with-trade domestic price of M_2 machines in Zend; this latter price, it must be remembered, will not be equal to the autarky price p_2^Z. Thus, with P_2 replaced in this way, equations (1), (3) and (4) of chapter 9 will apply to the present case. Now one obtains the international wage–profit frontier by eliminating the prices from the three wage–profit–price equations and the result of this elimination process is clearly quite independent of the particular interpretation given to those prices. It follows that the international wage–profit frontier given by (6) of chapter 9, which was obtained from (1), (3) and (4) of that chapter, is the international wage–profit frontier for the present case of M_2 machines being non-tradeable. This frontier being known, the determination of international equilibrium can proceed as in chapter 9.

It will be clear that, just as when all the commodities are tradeable, the determinants of the equilibrium values will be the available methods of production, the savings ratios, s^X and s^Z, and the exogenously determined wage and/or growth rates. It should be noted carefully that, just as in the case of a single, small economy, the methods of production of the non-tradeable commodity are as relevant to the determination of equilibrium as are those of the tradeable commodities and that the equilibrium price of the non-tradeable commodity, in the country in which it is produced, will be different from (in the present case, higher than) the corresponding autarky price.

If $p_1^X < p_1^Z$ then, it will be clear, a pattern 4 of production and trade must obtain, the international wage–profit frontier being given by (6) of chapter 9, with X and Z interchanged; the argument then proceeds as above.

M_1 non-tradeable

It was shown in chapter 8 that, with M_1 machines being non-tradeable, capitalists would adopt an M_2 specialisation if $P_2 > p_2$, while if $P_2 < p_2$ they would produce both M_1 machines and C, exporting the latter and importing M_2 machines. It follows that if P_2 is to be an equilibrium international price, it must lie between p_2^X and p_2^Z. If $p_2^X > P_2 > p_2^Z$ then the positive outputs in an international equilibrium will be C^X, M_1^X and M_2^Z, with C being exported from Xeres and M_2 machines being exported from Zend, i.e. a pattern 2 situation must obtain. On the other hand, if $p_2^X < P_2 < p_2^Z$, then the positive outputs will be C^Z, M_1^Z, M_2^X. This output pattern does not appear in Table 9.1 since, with all commodities tradeable, our 'machine comparative advantage' assumption implies that such a pattern will never be adopted. In the present context, however, since M_1 machines are non-tradeable, that assumption carries no such implication.

Suppose then that $p_2^X > p_2^Z$, so that an equilibrium pattern of output and trade must be of the pattern 2 kind. (If $p_2^X < p_2^Z$ the following argument applies with X and Z interchanged.) It was argued above that, with M_2 non-tradeable, relations (1), (3), (4) and (6) of chapter 9 applied, provided that the international price P_2 was replaced by the with-trade domestic price of M_2 machines in Zend. Now the same kind of argument may be applied again when M_1 machines are non-tradeable. Relations (1), (2) and (3) of chapter 9 will now hold, provided that the international price of M_1 machines, P_1, is replaced by the with-trade domestic price of M_1 machines in Xeres (the latter being less than p_1^X). The international wage–profit frontier given by (5) of chapter 9 is therefore the international wage–profit frontier for the present case, with M_1 machines being non-tradeable. This frontier being known, the determination of an international equilibrium can proceed as in chapter 9; the general conclusions reached will necessarily be simply those given above for the non-tradeable M_2 case.

C non-tradeable

As was seen in chapter 8, when C is non-tradeable capitalists will produce C and M_1 if $(P_2/P_1) > (p_2/p_1)$ but will produce C and M_2 if $(P_2/P_1) < (p_2/p_1)$. (It must be noted that here, and throughout this section, the symbols are used in the normal way, with C as the standard of value; in the corresponding section of chapter 8, by contrast, M_1 machines were taken as the standard of value.) Now our 'machine comparative advantage' assumption implies that $(p_2^X/p_1^X) > (p_2^Z/p_1^Z)$. It follows that if (P_1, P_2) are to be equilibrium international prices, they must satisfy $(p_2^X/p_1^X) > (P_2/P_1) > (p_2^Z/p_1^Z)$ and hence that the positive outputs in an equilibrium will be

C^X, C^Z, M_1^X, M_2^Z, with M_1 machines being exported from Xeres and M_2 machines being exported from Zend. This pattern of output and trade might perhaps be regarded as a 'mixture' of patterns 2 and 3 in Table 9.1; indeed, it could obtain at the singular point Y in Fig. 9.1(b), even with all commodities tradeable.

Since there will be four positive outputs in equilibrium, there are four corresponding wage–profit–price equations, the relative price of C in each country being, of course, a purely domestic price. On eliminating from these four equations the two domestic prices just referred to and the international relative price of M_1 and M_2 machines, one finds the international wage–profit frontier, which, in our usual notation, may be written as:

$$\left[\frac{m_1^X}{1+r^X}\right] - \left[\frac{w^X}{q^X - w^X}\right] = \frac{w^Z(1 + r^Z)}{(q^Z - w^Z)[m_2^Z - (1 + r^Z)]} \tag{6}$$

(At any combination of wage and profit rates satisfying (6), the corresponding international relative price for machines (P_2/P_1) is equal to each side of (6).) This international frontier having been found, the determination of international equilibrium may be carried out in the usual way.

It will be noted that, in the present case, the pattern of production and trade is determined by 'machine comparative advantage' alone, the conditions of production in the C industries (q^X and q^Z) and the exogenously given wage and/or growth rates being irrelevant. Nevertheless, the C production conditions and the exogenously given wage and/or growth rates, since they affect the position and shape of the international wage–profit frontier (6), do play a role in determining equilibrium international prices and the endogenously determined wage, profit and growth rates.

It may be concluded that, even in the presence of non-tradeable commodities, the determinants of an international equilibrium are the conditions of production of *all* commodities, the capitalists' savings ratios and the exogenously determined wage and/or growth rates.

MANY COMMODITIES, MANY COUNTRIES, MANY TECHNIQUES

It must now be considered how the foregoing analysis may be adapted to deal with the existence of many commodities, many countries and a choice of production methods in each country; in the interest of simplicity, the argument will be confined to the case of free trade, with all commodities tradeable and all countries growing at a common equilibrium rate. As a prelude, it will prove useful to recast our earlier analysis—for the case of three commodities, two countries and no choice of technique—in a somewhat different and perhaps rather more sophisticated form.

Reconsider, then, the analysis of international equilibrium in the case of the three commodities C, M_1 and M_2 and two countries, Xeres and Zend, in each of which there is one available method for the production of each commodity. One may now define an 'international technique' as a combination of three production processes, with one for each commodity, 'drawn from' either country. With three commodities and two countries, each providing one possible single-product process for the production of each commodity, there are clearly $2 \times 2 \times 2 = 8$ logically possible international techniques. Each technique, it must be noted explicitly, by involving the production of each commodity by a certain method, thereby involves it's being produced in a certain country, so that there is a particular location of production and pattern of trade implied by each international technique.

Now, of the 8 logically possible international techniques, two will be 'autarky' techniques, being composed of production processes which all belong to the same country; these may be ignored. Another two will each involve that M_1^Z and M_2^X are both positive and they may be ruled out—as irrelevant international techniques—by our usual 'machine comparative advantage' assumption. The remaining four international techniques involve precisely the production locations and consequent trade patterns that are shown on XYZ in Figs. 9.1 and in Table 9.1.

For each of the four relevant international techniques, there are three wage–profit–price equations, one for each commodity, which relate the international prices (P_1, P_2) and the wage and profit rates (w^X, r^X, w^Z, r^Z). Hence, by eliminating the prices (P_1, P_2) one can find the international wage–profit frontier for each international technique, linking (w^X, r^X, w^Z, r^Z); to each point, on each frontier, there will correspond particular international prices. The four-dimensional wage–profit frontier for each international technique may now be converted into a three-dimensional wage–growth rate frontier, by replacing r^X by (g/s^X) and r^Z by (g/s^Z), to yield a frontier on which any two of (w^X, w^Z, g) are inversely related.

All four wage–growth rate frontiers, one for each international technique, may now be drawn on the same three–dimensional diagram, with w^X, w^Z and g on the axes. The position and shape of each frontier will, of course, depend on the production coefficients for the methods involved and on the savings ratios, s^X and s^Z. Now, if any two of w^X, w^Z and g are exogenously determined, that international technique will be adopted which yields the greatest value for the third variable; associated with the equilibrium triplet (w_e^X, w_e^Z, g_e) will be the equilibrium international prices and the equilibrium profit rates. (If that triplet should lie on an intersection of distinct wage–growth rate frontiers, then we have an equilibrium at one of the singular points, X, Y, or Z, of Fig. 9.1.) Thus an international equilibrium will have been determined by the properties of the available production methods, the capitalists' savings ratios and the exogenously determined wage and/or growth rates.

It was seen earlier in this chapter that each of the patterns 1 to 4 of production and trade, i.e. each international technique, yields a three-dimensional consumption–growth frontier, relating (c^X, c^Z, g); it will be clear that these consumption–growth frontiers could all be drawn on the same diagram as the wage–growth rate frontiers and that each consumption–growth frontier would lie outside the corresponding wage–growth rate frontier (unless $s^X = s^Z = 1$). It would then not be difficult to show, in terms of the present analysis, how a competitive, capitalist equilibrium will not, in general, be optimal in terms of consumption and growth. This demonstration must, however, be left to the reader, as must a consideration of how tariffs could be analysed by appropriately modifying the four wage–growth rate frontiers, for it must now be shown how a greater number of commodities, countries and available processes can be allowed for.

More machines

Suppose first that, while there are still just two countries and no choice of technique within either country, there are n machines $M_1, M_2, M_3,$ $\ldots, M_{n-1}, M_n$. The M_1 machine is used in producing C, M_2 in producing M_1, M_3 in producing M_2, etc., while the M_n machine can be used to produce either M_{n-1} or M_n machines (cf. chapter 8). There being $(n + 1)$ commodities and two countries, there are clearly 2^{n+1} logically possible international techniques; two of them will be the autarky techniques which may be ignored. If it is now assumed that, in an obvious notation, $(m_{n-1}^X/m_n^X) > (m_{n-1}^Z/m_n^Z)$, i.e. that Xeres has the comparative advantage in M_{n-1} machines with respect to M_n machines, then all international techniques in which M_{n-1}^Z and M_n^X are positive may be ignored; there are 2^{n-1} such international techniques. Thus the number remaining to be considered is $(2^{n+1} - 2^{n-1} - 2)$.

For each relevant international technique, there will be $(n + 1)$ wage–profit–price equations (one for each commodity) relating the n international prices $(P_1, \ldots, P_n)$, the wage rates (w^X, w^Z) and the rates of profit (r^X, r^Z). The n prices may be eliminated to obtain, for each international technique, an international wage–profit frontier linking (w^X, r^X, w^Z, r^Z); this, in turn, may be converted into a wage–growth rate frontier by substituting (g/s^X) and (g/s^Z) for r^X and r^Z respectively. The argument then proceeds just as in the case of two machines and it will be clear that the general conclusion concerning the determinants of international equilibrium will be unaffected by the number of machines.

Alternative processes of production

Suppose now that, while there are only two countries as before, there are alternative methods of production available in each country, each method of production involving, of course, a particular type of machine. The number of logically possible international techniques may be very large indeed but that in no way alters the nature of the argument. For each one, the number of wage–profit–price equations will be one greater than the number of machine prices—since there must be an equation for C production as well as one for the production of each type of machine—and therefore the machine prices may be eliminated to yield an international wage–profit frontier. The latter may then be converted into a wage–growth rate frontier in the usual way. Thus no matter how many alternative methods of production and kinds of machine there may be, each logically possible international technique has its own three-dimensional (w^X, w^Z, g) frontier; all these frontiers may then be drawn on the same diagram and the properties of the international equilibrium be determined when any two of (w^X, w^Z, g) are given. (It may be noted that no mention has been made here of eliminating, as irrelevant, the 'autarky' techniques and any international techniques ruled out by comparative advantage considerations. Such a preliminary elimination would prove rather tedious in the present context and it is, in any case, not strictly necessary; the wage–growth rate frontiers for those international techniques will lie below the frontier for at least one other international technique and thus an 'irrelevant' technique will never be the equilibrium one.) Hence the determinants of international equilibrium continue to be the conditions of production, the capitalists' savings ratios and the exogenously determined wage and/or growth rates, no matter how many production methods and types of machine there may be.

Many consumption commodities

The above generalisations, while allowing the number of machines to be arbitrarily large, have still been based on the assumption that there is a single consumption commodity. It is, however, simple to allow for any number of consumption commodities provided that one may take as exogenously determined the *proportions* in which those commodities enter the real wage bundle in a given country; those proportions need not, of course, be at all similar as between countries.

Suppose, then, that in addition to the C commodity discussed so far, there are other consumption commodities $C_2, C_3, \ldots, C_N$. Let $\bar{w}_i^X$ represent the fixed ratio of consumption of C_i to consumption of C in the wage bundle of workers in Xeres. The real wage rate in Xeres will then be a bundle of N commodities which may be written as $w^X(1, \bar{w}_2^X, \ldots, \bar{w}_N^X)$, where w^X can both be interpreted as before and interpreted as an 'index' of the real wage rate. A similar notation can, of course, be introduced for Zend. An international technique will now be a set of processes for producing the N consumption commodities and the machines needed in that production. Taking C as the standard of value as before, there will now be $(N - 1)$ international prices of consumption commodities, in addition to all the machine prices. It remains true, however, that for each international technique, all the prices may be eliminated from the corresponding wage–profit–price equations to yield an international wage–profit frontier, which may, in turn, be converted into a wage–growth rate frontier linking (w^X, w^Z, g). The argument then proceeds as before. The effect on our general conclusion, of the introduction of many consumption commodities, is merely that to the set of determinants of international equilibrium must be added the proportions in which those commodities enter the wage bundles in Xeres and Zend.

Many countries

It may now be considered how the analysis can be extended to allow for an arbitrary number of countries. While both the number of commodities and the number of countries are now taken to be arbitrarily large, it should be noted that a sensible discussion of world trade has to be based on the assumption that the number of commodities is far greater than the number of countries; it would be mere idle speculation to consider the opposite case. While the number of countries in the world is of the order of two hundred, the number of commodities must run to the order of hundreds of thousands, provided that 'a commodity' is defined sufficiently narrowly that one may reasonably talk of its specific, technical conditions of production. One is, of course, at liberty to say that commodities can be classified into broad groups, such as primary materials, manufactures and services, but one cannot then sensibly talk of the coefficients of production for such 'aggregate commodities', as one needs to do for the purposes of theory. Nor are propositions concerning such broad aggregates likely to be of great help in understanding the trade of any particular country, which will always be trade in certain narrowly defined commodities.

Let there be k countries, then, where k is much smaller than the total number of commodities of all kinds. The existence of alternative production methods in each country is already allowed for, in that specific machines will be associated with particular, alternative methods of production. (Each method is still assumed to be of the circulating capital, single product type.) Let the proportions in which the consumption commodities enter the real wage bundle also be given for each country. The wage 'index', in terms of the C commodity, may be defined as w^j in country j, while the capitalists' savings ratio in that country may be denoted by s^j.

For each logically possible international technique, there will be a wage–profit–price equation for each commodity involved and it will therefore be possible to eliminate the prices to obtain the international wage–profit frontier for that international technique. That frontier can then be converted, by substituting (g/s^j) for each r^j, into a wage–growth rate frontier, which will define an inverse relation between any two of the variables $(w^1, w^2, \ldots, w^k, g)$. With any k of those variables exogenously determined, that international technique will be adopted which, under the pressure of competitive forces, maximises the value of the remaining variable. The equilibrium international technique will thus be determined and so, consequently, will be the international location of production of each commodity. Equilibrium international prices will also be determined, being those associated with the use of the equilibrium technique when the wage indices and profit rates are $(w_e^1, \ldots, w_e^k)$ and $(r_e^1, \ldots, r_e^k)$ respectively. The determinants of the international equilibrium will be the properties of the available methods of production, the capitalists' savings ratios, the proportions in which the consumption commodities enter the wage bundles in the k countries and the k exogenously given wage indices and/or growth rate.

It was stated above that the international location of production was determined by the argument there given; it must be noted both that that statement may need qualification and that, by contrast with our discussion of the two country case, nothing was said concerning the pattern of trade. These two points are closely related. With many more commodities than countries, it is quite likely that equilibrium prices, wage rates and profit rates will be such that capitalists in more than one country could profitably engage in the production of a given commodity. The precise location of production of that commodity will then not have been fully determined by our analysis; such a situation has already been met at each singular point Y in Fig. 9.1. Now suppose that a particular commodity is produced in more than one country and is also required for use in more than one country. (Any consumption commodity is likely to be used in more than one country and some machines may be so used.) In such a case, even if the locations of production and use are fully determined, the patterns of *trade* may not be, for it will still be open to question which source of supply is adopted by each set of capitalists using the given commodity. Further analysis of this point, which would perhaps necessitate consideration of transport costs, of trading institutions and of the historical development of links between particular countries, will not be pursued here.

SUMMARY

It was first shown how an 'international consumption–growth frontier' could be derived for any pattern of specialisation, for the case of two countries with a uniform growth rate. Such a frontier is dual to the corresponding wage–profit frontier, if the profit rates are set equal to one another. It was then seen that, with balanced trade, the determination of equilibrium consumption levels had in fact been implicit in the analysis presented in chapter 9. It was remarked that, in the simple case of given, equal growth rates in the two countries, all four logically possible combinations of consumption-optimal and non-optimal specialisations could actually occur, as could all four logically possible combinations of 'gain' and 'loss' from trade. (The comparisons involved were, of course, of a comparative dynamic nature.)

It was then shown that if the labour force growth rate in each of the two countries were positively related to the real wage rate (at least up to a certain level) then a unique international equilibrium, with a constant percentage rate of unemployment in each country, would exist provided that the capitalists' savings ratios were not 'too high'. Such an international equilibrium would yield both a higher real wage and a higher growth rate, in each country, than would autarky.

It was seen how the international equilibrium effects of a tariff could be analysed by considering the implied changes in the with-trade wage–profit frontiers: a tariff may or may not alter the equilibrium pattern of trade; it can be prohibitive, just as in the small economy case; it will change equilibrium international prices; and it will, for example, *lower* the equilibrium rates of profit and growth corresponding to given real wage rates. It was noted that the effect of a tariff on the 'gain from trade' is not known *a priori* and that the effects of other (non-tariff) trade policies can be analysed in a similar way to those of tariffs.

It was then shown that non-tradeable commodities could be introduced without affecting the conclusion that the proximate determinants of international equilibrium are the conditions of production, the capitalists' savings ratios and the exogenously given wage rate(s) and/or growth rate(s). It was noted that, as in the analysis of chapter 8, the production conditions for non-tradeables are just as important in determining international equilibrium as are those of tradeables and that trade affects the domestic relative prices of all commodities, both tradeables and non-tradeables.

The analysis was concluded by showing how the arguments of chapter 9 could be re-cast in terms of an 'international wage–growth rate frontier' and that this latter construction could be generalised to allow for many techniques, many commodities and many countries. It was remarked that the introduction of many techniques and many machines alters the method of analysis not at all and that the presence of many consumption commodities is equally unembarrassing *provided that* such commodities enter the real wage in given, fixed proportions. To allow for many countries does, however, affect the analysis more significantly, since the international location of production may well not be fully determinate: the same is true, but with even greater force, with respect to the precise pattern of trade flows.

AN INVITATION

While more general than that of earlier chapters, the analysis just presented is, of course, still based on a number of restrictive assumptions. Yet it is hoped that the reader will not only have absorbed the specific results established throughout this work but will also have acquired a 'feel' for the type of analysis presented. The reader is thus invited to generalise, to use, to extend and, indeed, to question that analysis in whichever way is appropriate with respect to each issue of interest within international trade theory. It is not merely fortuitous that no particular 'closure' of the theoretical system has been insisted upon; our objective has been only to establish an open-ended framework for the analysis of international trade amongst growing economies—a framework which different readers will choose to apply and to develop in different ways.

Our major general conclusion is that the principal *proximate* determinants of an international equilibrium are the alternative available methods of production, the capitalists' savings ratios and the exogenous data referring to real wages and/or the growth rate. It is to be expected—or, more cautiously, to be hoped—that on accepting the invitation to work within the suggested framework, the reader will find that that conclusion will need only to be qualified or modified and not to be abandoned.

SUBJECT INDEX

Aims of policy, not to be covertly recommended by the trade theorist, 93
Allocation of labour
in autarkic economy, 23–4, 33
in international equilibrium, 124, 125–8
may not be fully determinate, 128, 152

Balanced trade, 14, 50, 87, 90
in relation to consumption–growth frontiers, 50, 132

Capital goods
assumption of circulating capital goods not essential, 27–8
growing importance in world trade, 2
in H–O–S theory, 3–6
in long-period equilibrium, 8
international mobility consistent with international immobility of money capital, 13
Capital in H–O–S theory, 4–5
Capitalists' savings ratio, 25
effects on international equilibrium, 122, 123, 124, 132, 137–8
importance for consumption–optimality of choice of technique (or specialisation), 31–2, 53–4, 56–9, 133–4
Choice of specialisation, in a small economy
'alternative' method of analysis, 45–7, 55–6, 57–8, 80, 87, 95–6
as a choice of technique, 49
with given profit rate, 38–43
with given wage rate, 43–5
Choice of technique
and consumption, 31–2, 49–59, 96, 132–4
in autarkic economy, 28–31, 33
in open economy, 94–8, 149
Closure of system
given growth rate, in small economy, 26
given wage rate, in small economy, 25–6
in international equilibrium, 119–24, 147–8, 151
relative unimportance of particular closures adopted for exposition, vii, 26, 154

Comparative advantage in machine production, 115–18, 128, 143, 145, 146, 147, 148
Comparative dynamic nature of the analysis, 10–11, 35–6, 49–50, 59, 60–1, 72–3
Competition, 13, 34, 36, 109
Constant returns assumed throughout, 19, 34
Consumption, 9, 16, 32–3, 105–8, 150
in H–O–S theory, 6–7
Consumption–growth frontier
in autarkic economy, 25
in a small, open economy, 50–2, 55–6, 57–8, 74
international frontier, 131–2, 148

Determinants of international trade pattern, 16–17, 48, 65–7, 79–80, 83–7, 89, 108, 128, 141, 146, 148, 149, 151, 152, 154

Effective demand, 11–12
Effective protection, chapter 6 *passim*, 139–42
Employment
constant rates of unemployment in international equilibrium, 134–8
full employment not assumed, 12, 125
relative magnitudes of in trading economies, 126–8
and wages, 12, 26

Fixed capital, 27–8

Gain from trade
can be positive, zero or negative, 54–6, 57, 58–9, 107–8, 134
in a small economy, 49–59, 96
in international equilibrium, 132–4
may be ambiguous with a given wage, 57–8
may be increased or decreased by protection, 73, 142
Growth in H–O–S theory 5–6

Heckscher–Ohlin–Samuelson theory, 3–7

and capital, 4–5
and consumption, 6–7
and growth, 5–6
and primary inputs, 6
effect of positive profits on, 3
not firm foundation for modern trade theory, 7

Import quotas, 90–2
compared with tariffs, 91–2
International consumption–growth frontier, 131–2
International equilibrium, chapters 9, 10 *passim*
allocation of labour in, 124, 125–8
and consumption and gain from trade, 132–4
must involve semi-specialisation, 110–11
need not involve trade in all tradeable commodities, 114
and tariffs, 139–42
with constant rates of unemployment, 134–8
with given growth rates, 123–5
with given wage rates, 119–22
with many commodities, countries, techniques, 146–52
with non-tradeable commodities, 143–6
with one growth rate, one wage rate given, 122–3
International prices
affected by multiple exchange rates, 142–3
affected by tariffs, 141
induce trade (in absence of barriers to trade) if different from autarky prices, 37, 95, 112–19
need not lie between corresponding autarky prices in the trading economies, 116
and pattern of specialisation in a small economy, 41–2, 44–7
relation to wage and profit rates, 116–17
International wage–growth rate frontier, 147–51
International wage–profit frontier, 116–19
its significance for international equilibrium, 119–24, 140–2
with non-tradeable commodities, 144–6
with tariffs, 139–40

Long-period equilibrium, its definition and use, 8–9

Mobility (domestic) and immobility (international) of labour and of money capital, 13–14, 35, 109
Multi-commodity analysis, 98–9, 148–52

Multi-country analysis, 150–2
Multiple exchange rates, 87–90
and international equilibrium, 142–3

Non-tradeable commodities, 99–108, 143–6
and international equilibrium, 143–6
their production conditions affect – and their prices are affected by – trade, 101, 102, 104, 106, 108, 144–6
tradeable commodities may not be traded commodities, 114, 125–6

Prices
domestic prices made to diverge from international prices by tariffs, 60, 71, 76; by other trade policies, 92–3
relation to distribution under autarky, 22–3, 33
Primary inputs, 14–15
in H–O–S theory, 6
Production methods
assumed to differ between countries, 12–13, 15; not to differ, 115
choice between alternative methods, 28–31, 33, 94–8, 146–9
and pattern of trade in small economy, 41–7
Protection lowers the wage–profit frontier but may or may not lower the consumption–growth frontier, chapters 6, 7 *passim*

Rate of profit
effect on H–O–S theory, 3
equalised within countries but not between countries, 13, 109
relation to rate of growth, 25
'Ricardian' trade theory, 14, 105–6

Small economy, defined, 35
Steady growth analysis, 10–12, 14, 15, 34, 110
Subsidies, 78–82
combined with tariff in self-financing scheme of protection, 80–2
compared with production taxes, 83
compared with tariffs, 78–9
raise the wage–profit frontier, 79–80

Tariffs
cause domestic prices to diverge from international prices, 60, 71, 76
combined with subsidy in self-financing scheme of protection, 80–2
compared with quotas, 91–2
domestic price raising versus merely penalising tariffs, 69–70, 71–2

and the gain from trade, 73, 142
and international equilibrium, 139–42
lower the wage–profit frontier, 62, 64, 67, 69, 72, 75, 140
may or may not alter specialisation, 65–6, 67, 140–1
prohibitive, 62, 64, 67, 141
and revenue, 74–5
in a small economy, 60–76
use to protect an industry, 67–72; not always possible, 71
Taxes and trade, 82–7
Technical progress and why not discussed, 9–10
Transitions, not considered, 11, 36, 50, 59
Transport costs, 99, 152
Trends in world trade, 1–3

Von Neumann models, 9

Wage–profit frontier, 21–2, 28–31, 46–7
for small open economy, 46, 55–6, 57–8, 95–6
with multiple exchange rates, 88–90
with non-tradeable commodities, 101, 102, 104
with subsidies, 79–80
with tariffs, 61–2
with taxes, 83–6
see also International wage–profit frontier
Wage rate
equalised within countries but not between countries, 13
not driven to zero by unemployment, 12
with heterogeneous labour, 15